CW01269838

FICTION AND THE WEAVE OF LIFE

Fiction and the Weave of Life

JOHN GIBSON

OXFORD
UNIVERSITY PRESS

OXFORD
UNIVERSITY PRESS

Great Clarendon Street, Oxford OX2 6DP

Oxford University Press is a department of the University of Oxford.
It furthers the University's objective of excellence in research, scholarship,
and education by publishing worldwide in

Oxford New York

Auckland Cape Town Dar es Salaam Hong Kong Karachi
Kuala Lumpur Madrid Melbourne Mexico City Nairobi
New Delhi Shanghai Taipei Toronto

With offices in

Argentina Austria Brazil Chile Czech Republic France Greece
Guatemala Hungary Italy Japan Poland Portugal Singapore
South Korea Switzerland Thailand Turkey Ukraine Vietnam

Oxford is a registered trade mark of Oxford University Press
in the UK and in certain other countries

Published in the United States
by Oxford University Press Inc., New York

© John Gibson 2007

The moral rights of the author have been asserted
Database right Oxford University Press (maker)

First published 2007

All rights reserved. No part of this publication may be reproduced,
stored in a retrieval system, or transmitted, in any form or by any means,
without the prior permission in writing of Oxford University Press,
or as expressly permitted by law, or under terms agreed with the appropriate
reprographics rights organization. Enquiries concerning reproduction
outside the scope of the above should be sent to the Rights Department,
Oxford University Press, at the address above

You must not circulate this book in any other binding or cover
and you must impose the same condition on any acquirer

British Library Cataloguing in Publication Data
Data available

Library of Congress Cataloging in Publication Data
Data available

Typeset by Laserwords Private Limited, Chennai, India
Printed in Great Britain
on acid-free paper by
Biddles Ltd., King's Lynn, Norfolk

ISBN 978-0-19-929952-2

For Simona Bertacco

Acknowledgements

Literary aesthetics has been an interest of mine, though for much of the time on the back-burner, since my undergraduate years. I was introduced to aesthetics in an undergraduate course with Fred Beiser on Kant, Schiller, and Hegel, and my interest turned into something approximating a fixation during my first year of graduate school after a course with Brad Inwood on Aristotle's *Poetics*. It somehow took me another three years to discover that there is such a thing as contemporary philosophy of literature, and that it is a thriving and exciting area of philosophy. Sonia Sedivy helped me realize this, and she, along with Ronnie de Sousa, André Gombay, and Lubomír Doležel, were kind enough to allow me write a dissertation on the issues explored in this book. I am grateful to all of them. Ronnie reappeared four years later and read my typescript in its entirety. I benefited immensely from his comments and criticisms, and if he happens to read the final product I hope that he will see how much my arguments have changed, and, one hopes, improved on account of his uniformly sage suggestions. I taught for four years at Temple University, where I wrote many of the following pages, and my colleagues there were always willing to read and discuss my work. I am especially grateful to Phil Alperson, Noël Carroll, Susan Feagin (who has been helpful in more ways than I can recall), Kristin Gjesdal, Robert Guay, Espen Hammer, and David Wolfsdorf. I owe a very great deal to Joe Margolis, who I am confident will approve of little I say in this book, though I hope he will appreciate the spirit in which it was written. A special thanks is due to Simona Bertacco, Bernard Harrison (whose own work turned me on to the issues explored here and informs many of the following arguments), Wolfgang Huemer, and Luca Pocci, who have read virtually every word of this book. I owe Richard Eldridge a resounding word of thanks, and not only on account of the influence his work has had on my own. It was during a very pleasant walk in Cortina that he helped me to see that I had a book, nearly ready for submission, something I was more or less unaware of before that day. Since then he has helped with virtually every aspect of this project. Suffice it to say that this book would not exist had it not been for his interventions. I am also grateful to Peter Momtchiloff, Rupert Cousens, and Victoria Patton at OUP, who were always helpful and supportive (and apparently limitless in patience). Thanks as well to Hilary Walford, whose skillful editing helped rescue my writing from not infrequent spells of gracelessness and obscurity. If one recalls the line about Plato, footnotes, and the history of philosophy, I think it fair to say that the same is true of recent philosophy of literature and Peter Lamarque and Stein Haugom Olsen's *Truth, Fiction, and Literature: A Philosophical Perspective*. The influence of their book is omnipresent in the following pages—as it is virtually everywhere else in the debates I explore here—and it is thus fitting that I also acknowledge a considerable debt to their superb book.

An earlier and shorter version of Chapter 3 was published in *The British Journal of Aesthetics*, of Chapter 4 in the *Journal of Aesthetics and Criticism*, and of Section 5.1 in *Symposium*. Parts of the Introduction and Chapters 1 and 3 appeared in *The Literary Wittgenstein* and will appear in *The Oxford Handbook of Philosophy and Literature*. I thank Blackwell Publishers, Routledge, Oxford University Press, and La Société Canadienne de Philosophie Continentale for permission to reprint this material.

Contents

Introduction	1
1. The Loss of the Real	13
1.1. Indirect Humanism	18
1.2. The Sceptic's Recital	28
1.3. Literary Isolationism	36
2. Literature and the Sense of the World	50
2.1. The Picture of Paradox	52
2.2. The Paris Archive	60
2.3. Narrating the World	69
3. Beyond Truth and Triviality	81
3.1. Texts *as* Truths?	85
3.2. Mere Knowledge	99
3.3. Literature and the Fulfilment of Knowledge	112
4. The Work of Criticism	121
4.1. Interpreting Words, Interpreting Worlds	123
4.2. Interpretation and the Investing of Fiction with Life	136
4.3. Criticism and Cognitivism	141
5. The Fictional and the Real	146
5.1. The Threat of Panfictionalism	147

5.2.	The Limits of Make-Believe	157
5.3.	A Case for Openness	173

Conclusion 185

References 188
Index 199

Introduction

This book is a study of the relationship between literature and life—or, as it might be more fashionably put, it is a discussion of the connection between literary texts and 'extra-textual' reality. The first chapter acts as an introduction to the conceptual project of this book, and here I will just say a few words about what to expect in the following pages.

The term 'literature' is about as unruly as they come. It is used to designate everything from the sort of writing one finds in the Bible and Tacitus' *Histories* to Christopher Marlowe's plays and Ezra Pound's poetry. The sort of literature I am interested in here, and the sort one usually has in mind when writing on topics in literary aesthetics, is imaginative literature—works of *fiction*—and when I speak of literature it is always literature of the imaginative variety that I shall have in mind. Novels, short stories, plays, and much, though certainly not all, poetry are examples of imaginative literature in this sense (poetry is always imaginative but frequently not fictional; hence the qualification). As the institution of literature evolves, some argue that it will come to take under its extension narrative film, perhaps even television serials, though we shall have to wait to see whether the concept of literature will be able to bend that far. The problem I explore here can be applied to all these media, most, if not all, of the time. But my primary interest in this book is in the written word.

The problem that shall occupy me in this book concerns a tension that exists between two intuitions, a tension that I think lies very near the heart of the concept of the literary work of art. One intuition concerns the social and cognitive value of literature, and it tells us that literature offers us a window on our world. We might call this the *humanist intuition* and characterize it as the thought—or hope—that literature presents the reader with an intimate and intellectually significant engagement with social and cultural reality. It is the idea, one familiar to all of us in some respect, that literature is the textual form to which we turn when we want to read the story of our shared form of life: our moral and emotional, social and sexual—and so on for whatever aspects of life we think literature brings to view—*ways of being human*. The other intuition concerns how we understand the fiction that goes into a work of literary fiction. For it strikes us as equally intuitive to say that the imaginative basis of literary creation presents to the reader not her world but *other* worlds, what we commonly call 'fictional worlds'. If we think that literature tells us about our world, we have to make this square with the fact that we understand, and certainly read, literature as exempt from the task of worldly exegesis. A work of imaginative literature trades in aesthetic creation rather than factual representation. It speaks about people made of paper, who inhabit worlds made only of words. And from this it seems quite natural to conclude that literature is therefore essentially and intentionally silent about the way our world is, choosing instead to speak about worlds none of which are quite our own. The tension, then, is a matter of how we might reconcile these two intuitions, these basic visions we have of literature as somehow at once thoroughly our-worldly and otherworldly. This book is an attempt to offer such a reconciliation.

Though in recent scholarship there has been a renewal of interest in the humanist intuition, it is fair to say that common opinion has it that to discuss humanism is to conjure an old and annoying demon, one often thought to have been exorcized from literary aesthetics long ago. The reason for this, of course, is not that anyone believes that we have come to realize that literary fiction is after all irrelevant to life. It is because in many minds humanism is associated with a crude and antiquated tendency in the history of aesthetics and literary theory. In attempting this reconciliation, humanists have often been guilty of two sins, that of forging the connection to our world by taking literature to be a mimetic rendering of reality—thus relying on the now much disfavoured representational view of literature—and then that of going on to treat as the ultimate object of literary appreciation not the literary work of art itself but this world of which the text is thought to be just a mirror. There is an odd expression Derrida has popularized: 'il n'y a pas de hors-texte.'[1] Whatever this might exactly mean, if tamed into stating that, at least from the literary perspective, nothing outside the text matters, Derrida's curious proclamation brings to light a widely held claim. The extra-textual is often thought to be the extra-literary, beyond the reach of anyone who wants to illuminate the nature of what we witness when we look inside a literary work. To try to step from literature to the extra-textual is thus to take a step away from the very object of literary enquiry. And the humanist is often thought to be someone who has failed to learn this basic lesson, the dolt, in a word, who keeps trying to turn the *hors-texte* into the object of literary investigation.

The problem for the humanist runs deeper than literature's interest in the imaginary and the unreal. It is not only that when we look inside literary works we find descriptions of fictions. We also notice a conspicuous absence of all those tools, devices, and techniques we commonly take to be essential to the search for truth, knowledge, and like forms of worldly enlightenment: argumentation, the offering of evidence, the setting forth of 'the facts', the proffering of premises, the derivation of conclusions, and so. Needless to say, the ways in which works of history, philosophy, and science—paradigm cases of works of *enquiry*—make use of these devices and techniques varies considerably. It may even be the case that they are all, like literature, irreducibly narratological in form: this is a rather popular claim

---

[1] Derrida (1976: 158). In Anglo-American philosophy and literary theory this sentence is commonly translated as 'there is no outside the text'. It should probably be translated without the definite article, in which case it means something quite different: 'there is no outside-text', where *hors-texte* or 'outside-text' is a technical designation for a certain metaphysical notion that Derrida is trying to debunk. See Schalkwyk (2004: ch. 2) for an excellent discussion of this. Since the mistranslation helps my point along, I have chosen to stay with it.

in contemporary postmodern culture. But works of enquiry weave their narratives in ways very unlike works of literary fiction, and it is the particular way a narrative is woven that makes the difference here. Literature standardly constructs *fictional* narratives that have *dramatic* structures; works of enquiry standardly attempt to construct *factual* narratives that have *argumentative* (or evidentiary) structures. This would seem a rather important difference. And the challenge in defending the humanist intuition is to show that literary works can have a claim to cognitive value *in the absence* of those features of writing commonly taken to be the stuff of the pursuit of knowledge. For, in their absence, precisely what aspect of literary works do we point toward that justifies treating them as players in the pursuit of truth? What do we find *in* works of literature that entitles us to think that they even wish to be read for knowledge?

Few take this to be something worth lamenting, as though it reveals one of literature's secret shames. No one, as far as I am aware, claims that literature sees its labour as one of attempting to offer knowledge of the world yet is somehow constitutionally incapable of fulfilling its task. Nor is it usually thought that to call into question the humanist's view of literature is thereby to embrace a form of literary philistinism—namely, the picture of literary works as entertaining but ultimately trivial playthings. Since the rise of various brands of literary formalism and aestheticism, philosophers and literary theorists have done much to show that there is a powerful alternative to the humanist conception of literature, one that has an equal claim to being a defence of the value—or at least one of the core values—of literature. Philosophers of an anti-humanist bent do not deny that literary 'representations' (a term I shall return to sceptically throughout this book) are very often profound, perceptive, awe-inspiring, and so forth. The thought is rather that, while we will have a very hard time accounting for this profundity (and so on) in cognitive terms—say a profundity of *insight*—it is altogether easy to do so in *aesthetic* terms. It is also probably more natural, for literary works are, after all, artworks. Indeed, an aesthetic view of literature can even urge that it is to commit what Gilbert Ryle would call a category error to try to account for the value of literary content in cognitive terms: it amounts to a silly desire to carry over to aesthetic domains terms meant to account for the value of representations in philosophical and scientific domains.

Whether or not one quite agrees with this, it does have a certain appeal. For we have a vocabulary that works perfectly well for talking about artworks—an aesthetic vocabulary—and it is not altogether ridiculous to think that to apply the vocabulary we use to account for the value of works of enquiry also to literature is simply to misunderstand the nature of what we are talking about. At any rate, the possibility of offering a fully aesthetic theory of literature marks the presence of a more direct, and certainly less challenging, way to account for the value of literature. It is hard to imagine a humanist who has not at one time felt its appeal, who has not at least for a moment thought that she may have taken the wrong route to arrive at her defence of literature.

There is a more important reason it is so difficult to do justice to the humanist intuition these days. Virtually all the resources contemporary philosophy has given us for describing the 'inside' of literary works appear to make impossible the claim that we can find in them something sufficiently real to give sense to the humanist intuition. Before the twentieth century, the tradition of broadly humanistic philosophizing about art—with roots in Aristotle and extending through the German and English Romantic traditions—was canonical, though of course always with the occasional detractor. When philosophers spoke of art, there was, in addition to compulsory observations on the nature of beauty and other aesthetic features of art, almost always an important word offered on art's general cultural significance, on the ways in which works of art articulate an insight into our capacity to achieve freedom, attain moral selfhood, reveal the universal implicit in the particular, find meaning in a world without much of a point, and so forth.[2] But when philosophy took its initial steps toward the so-called linguistic turn of the

---

[2] See Davis (1996) and Weston (2001).

twentieth century, discussions of the nature of literature began to focus on the logic and semantics of literary language rather than on its power of cultural articulation, and in philosophical circles a very different habit of speaking about literature began to emerge. Perhaps the decisive first step in this shift was Gottlieb Frege's 1892 publication of *Über Sinn und Bedeutung*, in which we find claim that:

In hearing an epic poem we are...interested only in the sense of the sentences and the images and feelings thereby aroused. The question of truth would cause us to abandon aesthetic delight for the attitude of scientific investigation. Hence it is a matter of no concern for us whether the name 'Odysseus' has reference, so long as we accept the poem as a work of art.[3]

What we find announced here is a view of the language of literary works that has the consequence of severing whatever internal connection we once thought might exist between literary works and extra-literary reality. True, there are few Fregeans around today, at least in literary aesthetics, but the very general orientation towards literature we find in *Über Sinn und Bedeutung* is still with us. Frege's view of literature as a sort of pure 'sense' language has not aged well (in fact, it may not even be Frege's view, but that is another story). Literature does, on many views, have truth and reference, just of a rather deviant sort. What we find in the tradition that arose after Frege is that the notions of truth and reference have been relocated to the *fictional* dimension of literature, in order to explain the ways in which works of literature function to 'refer' to and state 'truths' about fictional worlds. Thus these notions no longer serve the traditional humanistic purpose of marking the means by which literary works speak about reality. In this respect, while philosophers have recovered from Frege a notion of 'literary reference', the wedge Frege drove between literature and truth—indeed between literature and the world—is still very firmly in place.

[3] Frege (1970: 63).

The consequence of this is that literature is effectively made mute about the stirrings of extra-literary reality. What we find in this shift in twentieth-century literary aesthetics from traditional humanistic concerns to an overriding interest in the logic and semantics of fictional discourse is that philosophy has developed a vocabulary for speaking about literature that has made it seemingly impossible to give sense to the humanist intuition. What the philosopher of literature presently has at her disposal is a constellation of extremely sophisticated theories of fiction nearly all of which make it impossible to see how we might speak like humanists. In practically all the popular theories of fiction we see a commitment to the old Fregean move of denying that literature has real-worldly truth and reference (I shall argue for this in the following chapters; the reader will have to take it on credit here). The upshot of all this is that it gives the air of nonsense to the idea that literary language might actually be able to tell us something of cognitive significance about the world. For if it does not speak about reality—if it sends its words and descriptions to fictional rather than real addresses—how could it possibly be revelatory of reality? In this respect, the problem for the humanist is not merely that literary works refuse to use the tools of enquiry to build support for their claims. *Literature does not even make claims about reality*, so there is really nothing for it to support. At any rate, this is the picture of literary language we have inherited from the last century.

This is probably one of the reasons why humanists are often thought to endorse a very naive view of literature, identifying the object of literary attention with the *hors-texte* rather than literary content itself. Given the notion of fiction with which so much contemporary philosophy operates, we can see why humanists often make this mistake. If what we have to say about literary fiction is that it concerns fictional worlds, or in any case worlds other than our own, then the idea of finding reality disclosed *in* a literary work is made utterly mysterious. Accordingly, it appears obligatory to look outside the text to establish a connection between literature and reality. But, once we do, we have lost touch with the literary and thus the very thing the humanist is trying to explain. Given what philosophy tells us it means for a text to be fictional, for a use of language to be literary, it is very hard to see how we might defend the intuitions of the literary humanist.

This is the challenge I shall address in this book. What I wish to show is that we can be humanists without the sin. Humanists need not be the reactionary outsiders they are commonly thought to be and indeed often have been. As I will argue, the humanist intuition can sit quite comfortably with those theories of literature commonly taken to reveal its implausibility (after a bit of tinkering, needless to say). And so a properly developed theory of humanism, far from demanding that we abandon standard ways of speaking about the nature of literary fiction, can be seen as offering a significant and attractive addition to the various critical and theoretical vocabularies we already possess.

I hope to give a sense of how powerful the arguments against the humanist view of literature are but also to bring to light how the philosopher beholden to it might respond to them. More precisely, I shall argue that we must accept that literature's particular manner of engaging with reality is *sui generis*, so much so that it constitutes its own form of insight and worldly investigation. This implies, among others things, that we should abandon what we might call the *philosophy-by-other-means* view of literature, and in general any defence of literary humanism that attempts to model literature on a theory of how *other* sorts of texts can have cognitive value, say by showing them to mimic philosophical works, perhaps by being a thought experiment in literary disguise, a sort of dramatic 'proof', an exercise in moral reasoning by example, and other similar things we in no obvious sense find when we look inside the majority of literary works. In making a case for this, I shall argue that literature's cognitive achievements are intimately bound up with its artist and aesthetic—especially *dramatic*—achievements. Humanists need not turn their backs to the specifically literary dimension of works of fiction when defending the cognitive value they believe many of them put on offer. Rather, humanist musts embrace this dimension, for it is here that literary works effect their particular enlightenment.

In the first chapter I set up the challenge of offering such a reconciliation between these two intuitions about the nature and value of the literary artwork. I introduce here the sceptic, himself a fiction but a fiction whose voice will draw together the most powerful reasons available for doubting that this reconciliation is possible. The structure of the sceptic's argument is quite simple, though its consequences are severe. He begins by telling us that the humanist must accept the following constraint: the humanist must prove that the value he wants to attribute to a literary text—namely, insights into the way our world is—is an actual property of the text itself. If he does not respect this constraint, the sceptic will show us that the humanist will fail to identify a proper *literary* value and thus will default on his promise to tell us something about the nature of literature. But, if the humanist accepts this constraint—and the sceptic will show us that he must—his intuition begins to look incoherent. We might recall a line from Shakespeare's *A Midsummer Night's Dream* that is frequently enlisted in this debate, a line that declares a basic truth about literary creation: 'And as imagination bodies forth the forms of things unknown, the poet's pen turns them to shape and gives to airy nothing a local habitation and a name.' The sceptic charges that it is utterly mysterious what it could mean to claim that we can see something real in this 'airy nothing' literature presents to view. If the humanist must locate reality within the literary work, and if the literary work brings only fictions, airy nothings, to view, the sceptic claims that humanism is hopelessly senseless.

In the second chapter I begin my defence of humanism against the sceptic's challenge. This chapter is an exploration of the linguistic and semantic considerations that make humanism seem so implausible. The sceptic's arguments make it look as though humanism is best described as built upon paradox, a desire to understand literature in terms of precisely what literature turns out to be contrasted with: a vision of the way the world is. I claim that the central reason we are inclined to think humanism paradoxical is because it shocks many of our more general linguistic intuitions, intuitions the sceptic exploits in his recital. To the extent that a work of imaginative literature represents anything, it represents fictions (namely fictional worlds). Yet one of the most common beliefs we have is that language fundamentally connects to reality by way of linguistic representation. In other words, it appears that literature's refusal to represent reality places a wedge between its words and reality. The claim I pursue in this chapter is that the humanist can embrace this (as it is often called) 'representational divide' that runs between literature and life. If literature does not represent reality, I argue that it plays a crucial role in the construction of those narratives in virtue of which we give sense to our characteristically human practices and experiences. Literature is in effect an archive of these narratives, a storehouse of the various ways we have developed for giving expression to the way our world is and our particular ways of finding ourselves within it. In this respect literature reveals itself to enjoy a certain priority to representation, for its presentation of human practice constitutes our sense of—rather than mirrors—those very practices. Accordingly, the humanist can argue that literature's relation to the world is better understood as *foundational* rather than representational, consisting in literature's ability to bring before us narratives that hold in place and give structure to our understanding of large expanses of cultural reality.

What this chapter offers is a model for making sense of the claim that literature can present our world to view. But the humanist needs more than this. He needs not only a linguistic but also an *epistemic* account of literature's capacity to reveal reality. Any form of humanism worth its name must capture the intuition that literature offers cognitive rewards to the careful reader; that one can *learn* from literary works of art. The question of the cognitive value of literature is the central challenge in the development of a serviceable model of humanism, and it is also the most difficult to answer. The sceptic has powerful arguments to the effect that, even if it is true that literature can bring our world to view, literature contributes nothing to our knowledge of this world in its act of presentation. In fact, we will see that the most we can say is that literature *presupposes* rather than *imparts* knowledge of the world. I argue in Chapter 3 that this is no loss, indeed that the traditional humanistic search for so-called knowledge through literature seriously miscasts the role literature can play in intellectual life. Knowledge specifies a certain conceptual relation to the world. What must be added to knowledge is an awareness of the *role* a piece of knowledge plays in our social and cultural practices: a sense of the connection between knowledge and those forms of human activity and response through a piece of knowledge is naturally expected to express itself. Literature takes this as its cue, exploring the real by tracing the link between the conceptual and the cultural. If this is so, though not trading in knowledge, literature turns out to offer what is best described as a *fulfilment* of the knowledge we bring to it, a completion of our understanding of how our concepts and words function to unite us with others and our world.

In the fourth chapter I turn to a consideration of the central role of interpretation in forging the connection between literature and life developed in the previous chapters. Recent approaches to interpretation tend to focus too narrowly on the *language* of literary works, developing theories that shed light on how we assign a determinate meaning to some ambiguous or otherwise semantically curious feature of a literary work. Though a fully developed theory of interpretation certainly must address this, meaning in literary-critical contexts is frequently much more complex than this. When we speak of meaning in literary-critical contexts, we are typically concerned not primarily or especially with the *signification* of the language of a literary work but rather with *significance* of the fictional worlds the text brings to view. The search for literary meaning is in large part the struggle to render explicit the import, the consequence, of the worlds that literary works bring to view. I argue that interpretation of this variety brings to light something quite extraordinary. The process of rendering explicit literary meaning reveals a certain way of investing fiction with life—namely, by placing the imagined lives we find in literary works within larger contexts of human activity. It is by way of the interpretative act of situating fictions in a critical context that specifies how they are 'about' or 'mean' something of general, and very much real, consequence that we can see how the bridge between the fictional and the real is built.

With the argument of the fourth chapter I will have made my case for humanism. I use the fifth and final chapter to offer some general observations on the nature of fiction. I discuss two positions that bring to view popular ways philosophers approach the notion of fiction: postmodern 'panfictionalism' (the idea that all forms of discourse are in the end fictional) and the analytic modelling of fiction on games of make-believe. Both of these approaches, though in very different ways, represent a tendency that I think is in large part responsible for the general disinterest in the question of literary humanism since the 1960s. The problem concerns how we should understand the nature of what is often called 'the fictive stance',[4] the basic attitude we assume when we appreciate textual content as fictional. The tendency is one of treating the fictive stance as by nature a turning-away from or inherently opposed to an appreciation of reality. Each of these theories, though again in quite different ways, gives expression to the idea, a mistaken one, that one and the same stance cannot have both the fictional and the real as its object. In discussing these theories I shall bring to light a few important restrictions on how we should understand just what we are saying when we describe literary content as fictional. I conclude this chapter by arguing that, if we look outside literature and examine other cultural practices that make use of fictions, we can see that, far from standing in a relationship of mutual antagonism, we have a general understanding that fictions can, and are regularly enlisted to, embody various regions of human experience. From here it will be a short step back to the question of literary humanism and a few concluding words on what it means to describe the theory offered in this book in terms of a concrete stance we can take towards the literary work of art.

---

[4] A phrase Lamarque and Olsen (1994) have popularized.

1

The Loss of the Real

What we might call the 'humanist intuition'—the conviction, however imprecise and pre-theoretical, that works of literary fiction can illuminate reality—has been with us in one guise or another since Aristotle wrote his *Poetics*, nearly as long as the Western literary tradition itself. Though only rudimentarily developed, we find there the basic idea that literature represents generalized features of life; that it deals with, to put it simply, *how we humans are*.[1] The humanist intuition will probably strike many of those uninitiated in contemporary philosophy and theory of literature as obvious, perhaps even bordering on a platitude. I would venture that, to most sensitive but non-academic readers of literature, nothing would seem particularly controversial in the claim that great literature is a mouthpiece of social and cultural reality: what we look to when we want to find a direct expression of its 'living spirit', as Schiller might say. And most of us, I will venture further, would be genuinely taken aback to find that the dominant theories of literature either leave no room for a humanist view of literature or—worse still for the intuitions of the uninitiated—spend a good amount of

---

[1] Of course, Aristotle had no notion of a position called 'humanism'. But his *Poetics* is often taken to be the first expression of the basis of a humanistic account of literature. The birth of what we now refer to as literary humanism is probably the famous passage in the *Poetics* (running from 1451^a38 to 1451^b12), in which Aristotle claims that, since *poiesis* deals with the general (*katholou*) rather than the particular, it is more like philosophy than history. He ends the argument by explaining that this universal concerns 'the sorts of things people may say or do necessarily or for the most part'—*how we humans are* in this sense.

time trying to show it to be an incoherent and indeed anti-literary position.[2]

As anyone with even a modest knowledge of contemporary literary theory has probably learned, calling oneself a humanist in literary circles resonates in much the same way as calling oneself a Cartesian dualist does in philosophical circles: certainly there are a few around, but the very label has the air of running conservatively counter to contemporary trends and positions. More frightening still for the uninitiated, if we look through the history of literary theory, we find that there are actually good reasons for this. The traditional homes of humanism have been either rather simple-minded and now outdated forms of biographical criticism and various other 'the life and times of the author' interpretative strategies—the old idea of *l'homme et son œuvre*—or a sort of literary metaphysicalism that sought Essences, Truths, and Universals in such a way that they often appear more akin to mysticism than genuine theory.[3] However commonplace the lay commitment to a humanistic view of literature may be, it is hard not to be left with the impression that humanism

---

[2] Tony Davis (1996) offers the most sustained account of the history of humanism and the variety of ways in which it has come under attack in postmodern, neo-marxist, and poststructural thought, especially in those areas of literary and cultural theory that are beholden to such thought. Terry Eagleton's various criticisms of forms of literary humanism (1997) are still worth reading. More recently, Tzvetan Todorov (2002) has written an intriguing study of the legacy of humanist thought about culture and art. For influential attempts to defend a version of humanism in contemporary analytical aesthetics (where 'humanism' tends to mean something *very* different from what it does in contemporary literary theory and cultural studies), see Novitz (1987); Harrison (1991); Lamarque and Olsen (1994); Nussbaum (1995); and Lamarque (1996, in Kieran 2006). More generally, one can find a commitment to what I am describing as a humanistic theory of literature in Cavell (1979; 1987), Eldridge (1997; 2001; 2003a), Freeland (1997), Carroll (in Levinson 1998), Gaut (in Levinson 1998, 2003), Kieran 2006), John (1998, in Gaut and Lopes 2001); Farrell (2004); and Kieran (2005).

[3] We can see this in many of the formulations of the 'concrete universal' given by the followers of New Criticism, and it might be best seen in Cleanth Brooks's idea (1968) of 'the eternal'. The same can be said of the so-called Scrutinists' (followers of F. R. Leavis) notoriously vague notion of 'life' as an indefinable and basic presence in literary texts. Together the New Critics and the Scrutinists represent the last major literary-critical humanisms of the last century (see Eagleton 1997), and both were effectively dead by the late 1960s, when poststructuralism swept through literary theory.

has not been done justice in the maze of contemporary literary theory.

Philosophy has not been much kinder to the humanist intuition than literary theory has been. If humanism (or a picture of literature's value that amounts to it) is as old as Aristotle, anti-humanism reaches back even further. The idea that literature is revelatory of reality has been attacked since Plato's famous anti-literary fulmination in the *Republic*. The fear that informs his arguments stems from his insight, a reasonable one itself, that there is something genuinely odd about literature.[4] Literature speaks our language, as it were. It borrows our words and grammar, our idioms and cultural references. But it does very strange things with these words. In literature the rails of reference run not from word to world but from word to chimeras, creatures of an author's imagination. And the natural conclusion might well appear to be that literature therefore talks quite literally about nothing, that it is a mere *flatus vocis*. For Plato the humanist intuition would suggest a rather serious case of ontological confusion, a sort of feeble-mindedness in which one has been tricked by literature into taking the unreal for the real, and so morally and intellectually dangerous for this reason.[5]

Plato's basic reason for rejecting the humanist intuition is neither antiquated nor unusual. Some of the major philosophical movements of the twentieth century have echoed Plato's argument. To take an obvious example, the philosophy of the Vienna Circle, and much of the subsequent verificationist and positivistic philosophy it gave rise to, had it that any use of language that is not reducible to the physical (empirical) mode of speech—in essence, any use that is not reducible to a description of some feature of the actual world—is meaningless. Literature, along with the arts in general, was thus relegated to the status of beautiful fluff and pomp: it might speak volumes to our

---

[4] Plato spoke not of literature but of *poesis*, 'poetry', in the expansive Attic sense of the term that denotes much of what the English term 'literature' does.

[5] A line of thought that underlies his arguments beginning at *Republic* X 595 with: 'Poetical imitations are ruinous to the understanding of the hearers, unless they possess the true nature of the originals as an anecdote.'

purely aesthetic sensibilities but it says nothing of genuine cognitive significance.

Humanism, we are beginning to see, is as controversial as it is intuitive. This chapter is an examination of what produces the controversy. Here I will give shape to the anti-humanist voice against which I will develop my theory of humanism in the following chapters, offering the sceptic a stage before trying to respond to his charges.[6] What we will see is that far from being a literary philistine, the sceptic appears to have both literature and reason on his side. The arguments the sceptic sets forth here pose a genuine threat to the humanist intuition. Indeed, they reveal something deeply puzzling about the idea that literature can or ever wishes to be revelatory of reality. The remainder of the book is an attempt to dispel this puzzlement.

Before I begin I need to give substance to the idea of literary humanism as I will develop it in the following chapters. The term 'humanism' has an extraordinary range of application and a long, varied history, not unlike the term 'realism' in philosophy. Many, indeed most, of the senses associated with this term have little to do with the use it has assumed in contemporary Anglo-American philosophy of literature. As philosophers of literature have recently begun to defend it, humanism has nothing to do with the odd beliefs of the old Italian *umanisti*, the 'politics' of liberal humanism, the view that 'man is the measure of all things', that human values are 'universal', or any of the other senses it has assumed in the many cultural and intellectual movements that since the Renaissance have made use of the designation.[7] It marks in literary aesthetics a very modest proposal: that there is an important link between literature and life, and that this link, whatever it may precisely consist

---

[6] My construction of the sceptic's position here is built out of problems that arise in almost all the core areas of the philosophy of literature. Each of the problems the sceptic draws on—questions concerning the nature of literary language, truth and reference, cognition—call out for closer examination. This is the work of the following chapters.

[7] See the introductions to Harrison (1991) and Lamarque (1996) for statements of literary humanism that have been influential in contemporary philosophy of literature. I am indebted to each here.

in, accounts for one of the central reasons we value literature. It is strange that such a humble claim might produce such controversy and require so much defence, but, as we will see, it has and continues to do so.

Yet what does it mean to assert such a link between literature and life? It means that we have grounds for claiming that part of the project of many (though certainly not all) literary works is to articulate an insight into some fairly specific region of human experience and circumstance. Though it is true that works of literary fiction trade in the unreal, in the imaginative creation of people and places that manifestly are not, the humanist still wants to claim that the content of literary works is not only, if you will, *fictional-worldly* but in some significant respect also *our-worldly*. The humanist wants to assert that through works of literature the significance of very real human experiences, practices, and institutions can be revealed when they were once mysterious or obscure; that a grasp of reality can be gained from close reading (hence literary *humanism*, for the claim is that literature speaks to human reality). The humanist means nothing metaphysical, implies nothing foundationalist, when he speaks of 'reality'. He gestures only toward the everyday world we inhabit—that is, the world of actual human experience and action—and from which we often distinguish with ease the fictional worlds we find in literary works. Thus the literary humanist is committed to the view that there is something common to both the world of (the fictional character) Bartleby and that of the audience reading *Bartleby the Scrivener*, and that this commonality consists in more than that the readers and the literary work merely share the same language, as though they part worlds when questions arise of what we and this work use language to talk about. Rather, the humanist will argue that at some significant level they both talk about the *same* world. And, as we will see, a viable theory of literary humanism will urge that this connection, whatever it may consist in, allows us to say what is either denied or nearly impossible to make sense of within the framework of much contemporary philosophy of literature and literary theory: that, far from appealing to exclusively 'textual' interests or inviting us only to play games of make-believe and the like, literary experience may be a direct appreciation of and engagement with the real world.

1.1. INDIRECT HUMANISM

The idea of 'directness' in the above description of humanism is paramount, and in the following two sections I will show exactly why the literary humanist must embrace it. If a picture of humanism is direct it will promise to secure the intuition that literary texts connect us to reality by locating the our-worldly, in some yet unspecified sense, immediately *within* the text. It will argue that reality can be a proper feature of literary content itself, that we can identify the real in the very words that make up a work of literature. It is perhaps hard to see what all this might mean. What could it possibly mean to say that literary works, engaged as they tend to be in fictional discourse, can in any direct or immediate respect be *about* reality, have reality *within* them?

In contrast to this view, in this section I describe what I will refer to as 'indirect humanism', a position that on the face of it is much weaker and much more sensible. The indirect humanist accepts that literary content is thoroughly fictional—that reality is, so to speak, always extra-literary—but attempts to bring literature to bear on the our-worldly by exploring our ability to *apply* aspects of the content of a literary work to extra-textual reality. Thus the reader builds the bridge between fiction and reality and so unites what the work itself cannot.

What I am calling indirect humanism marks the most common (and arguably intuitive) way of addressing the problem of the relation between literature and reality. Indeed, there are a considerable number of philosophers who appear to have no trouble at all claiming what I have just said is so difficult to claim—namely, that literary content is both thoroughly fictional *and* capable of revealing reality. As we will see, indirect humanism captures an unquestionably significant social and moral value of the institution of literature. The problem is that it is very difficult to tell what precise theoretical work we can do with the indirect humanist's insight. As we often find it, it is unclear whether an author promoting a position of this sort offers it as an observation of one of the social values of literature or as an identification of a proper humanistic *literary* value. As we shall see, this is the crucial point. If expressed as only the former, it is unexceptionable. The difficulty lies in treating it as an account of *literary* value, of the significance of what we find *within* literary works. The question humanism hangs on is whether literary works *themselves* can be revelatory of reality, and, as I shall argue here, the indirect humanist is bound to fail to answer this—in fact, he avoids rather than responds to the question itself. What we shall ultimately see is that the difficulty the indirect humanist faces shows us exactly what is at stake in developing the humanist intuition.

The sort of argument typically offered for a version of what I am calling indirect humanism is gracefully simple. It asks us to admit something few of us would deny: that literary works can at least invite modes of reflection, simulation, and imagination that can in turn lead us to a better understanding of our world.[8] If we want to find a way of capturing the conviction that we are put in touch with reality through literature, it seems quite natural to begin by trying to develop the idea that literature can illustrate *possibilities*; that it can offer a sketch of how, for example, rage can undo reason (say in Euripides' *Medea*) or a way in which we might see modern technology and perversion as growing out of one another (say in J.G. Ballard's *Crash*). We latch on to what might be called the 'modal dimension' of literary involvement, to its ability to present a *possible* way of conceiving experience, and look here

---

[8] As Eileen John felicitously puts it, 'even those who doubt that art is a source of knowledge generally grant that is a source of cognitive stimulation. To be cognitively stimulating means at the very least to prompt activities in conscious life: thoughts, feelings, perceptions, and desires' (John, in Gaut and Lopes 2001: 33). This is as good a characterization of the popular approach I am calling 'indirect humanism' as one can find. I take the argument I offer in this chapter to function as criticism of any view that grounds humanism on what John describes as cognitive stimulation.

to ground the connection between the 'world' generated by a work of literary fiction and the real world. As Kendall Walton reminds us: 'perhaps fiction is more often a means of performing other illocutionary acts—suggesting, asking, raising an issue, reminding, encouraging to act—than a means of making assertions' about the world.[9] It is not that literature, trading as it does in fictions, *tells* us how the world is. But it can suggest ways of regarding it, presenting us with new possibilities of worldly understanding and involvement.

It is easy to give substance to this line of thought. We begin by noticing that literature, while talking about fictions, is nevertheless able to offer—put vaguely at first mention—conceptions, stances, and perspectives. They are, in their proper literary mode of presentation, perspectives on purely fictional states of affairs. But when we read a work of literature, we are drawn into its perspective, we think from within it (the Underground Man's view of the satisfaction to be derived from suffering in *Notes from Underground*, for example). Once we have done this, we need only state the incontestable fact that the reader can then take the conception we find in a story and use our reflective and imaginative capacities to transform it into a tool for approaching reality. As Catherine Wilson puts it, giving substance to such a line of thought requires only that the reader '(a) recognizes the conception presented in the novel as superior to his own and (b) adopts it, in recognition of its superiority, so that it comes to serve as a kind of standard by which he reviews his own conduct and others'.[10]

One might object that many literary works do not offer anything like *a* stance on, or *a* clearly articulated conception of, experience (for example, James Joyce's *Finnegan's Wake*), and that, of those that do, we often find, for reasons moral and otherwise, that we would not want to turn the perspective they offer into a way of regarding worldly affairs (Henry Miller's view of sexuality in *Tropic of Cancer*). But notice how flexible the above line of reasoning is. All that is

---

[9] Walton (1990: 78).   [10] Wilson (1983: 495).

crucial to the indirect humanist's position is the claim that we can treat literature as offering the raw material out of which we can build new ways of understanding our world. The indirect humanist can discard the idea that literature leads us to life by way of offering distinct and morally (and so on) attractive conceptions of experience, and in its place he can put all the emphasis on what *we* can take out of our imaginative participation in fictional worlds. Gregory Currie offers one such expression of this approach:

A really vivid fiction might get you to revise your values. Sometimes we suspect that our values are the wrong ones, and we may then desire to value differently. But fictions serve not only to change our current values; they can, more modestly, help us to reinforce or test our commitment to those own values... Fictions can help here by inviting us to imagine ourselves more committed than we really are to our values and then to see ourselves, in imagination, flourishing as a result.[11]

And Lamarque and Olsen characterize (without endorsing) this line of reasoning well when they write:

Through reflecting on certain conceptions in works of fiction, we learn to reflect with those conceptions in other contexts. Similarly by adopting certain points of view towards imaginary states of affairs, under the direction of the storyteller, we might come to adopt those same points of view in comparable situations elsewhere.[12]

There is an important point in all these claims, an intuition that reflections of this sort capture remarkably well. 'Real' life rarely presents moral (or social, psychological, and so on) circumstance with the power and exactness of detail we find in works of literary fiction, and so novels offer us an opportunity to explore what life never quite gives us—or not, at any rate, as risk-free as literature does. None of us, one would hope, has ever witnessed a lynching. Yet, for that reason, none of us has been given the occasion to examine the shock of one, and so to engage in that refinement of moral response, of ideas of human dignity, of commitments to

[11] Currie (1995: 254–5).   [12] Lamarque and Olsen (1994: 136).

social change, that would naturally arise from witnessing something horrible of this order. It is a good thing that life rarely compensates for this lack. But it is also fortunate that we do not remain altogether innocent for it. We can, for example, read James Baldwin's 'Going to Meet the Man', and thus find occasion to examine, through our imaginative involvement with Baldwin's creation, the possibility of such an event, the significance it would carry for the entire spectrum of moral, social, and philosophical concerns that such a horror would touch upon. In short, though speaking about fictions, literature can play an important role in prodding us to examine questions of vital worldly interest, and the indirect humanist is surely right to insist on this. Literary works do not need to answer these questions if we are to find a way to connect them with life; they do not even need to raise the questions themselves. It is enough that they give us an occasion for this sort of exploration, a ground upon which to carry it out. And this exploration, of course, is not just for the reader's private enjoyment. Moral philosophy, for fairly obvious reasons, could make great use of such a practice, as could any area of human concern that requires exempla, illustrations, and anecdotes.

It is difficult to exaggerate how frequently one runs into claims like the above. Indeed, in the light of some of the more rigidly formalist theories of art and literature, it might be worth shouting the indirect humanist's argument. But thinking that we can turn this way of expressing the humanist's intuition into a viable theory of literary humanism is another matter altogether. Turning the above reflections into a genuine humanistic theory of literature requires showing: (i) that this act of imaginative and reflective involvement provides us with new ways of approaching reality, and (ii) that this says something about what we find in literary works and hence the nature of the literary. Few will deny (i). Indeed it would be silly to deny it: it would amount to claiming that we *cannot* apply the conception found in a work of art to the real world, and I have no idea how—or why—one would argue this. As we will see, (ii) is the essential condition, and the problematic one, for it is easy to show that it is untenable. In fact, the sceptic will show us that the indirect humanist's thesis reduces to a near platitude: that from the literary point of view it is just a grand way of recording the dull fact that novels, at least interesting ones, make us think. The important question is *what* we think about when we think about a literary work. And the sceptic argues that the answer to this question is that it is the world *only at the expense of the work*. The sceptic argues, in short, that we lose the literary if we try to unite it with the worldly as the indirect humanist does.

The sceptic's argument is simple. If literary texts offer suggestions, if they whisper possibilities and hint at new ways of approaching reality, on this indirect model it will always be the world that answers and never the literary work; it will always be reality (or our consideration of it) that determines whether the conceptions and perspectives we find in literature can be turned into cognitively adequate, world-directed stances. The indirect humanist admittedly concedes so much. But he fails to see the consequence of this admission—namely, that, when we consider these new ways of perceiving and knowing reality that we develop out of our encounters with literary narratives, we have turned away from precisely that to which we want to be brought closer: an understanding of the literary work and the array of ways in which we encounter *it* (rather than some external thing to which it might lead us).

Literary texts obviously do present the reader with objects of contemplation: the world of the story.[13] But beyond what is asserted, proposed, and stated in the literary work *about the world of that work*, a literary work does not provide a further claim to the effect that 'this is how the world is as well'. We may of course take what we find in a literary text and ask whether it holds true in the real world, whether, if we apply it there, we can acquire a better perspective of worldly affairs. But as soon as we have done this we

---

[13] As Terrance Diffey puts it, 'we cannot claim to have learned anything [from literature] unless we know that an *additional* premise is true, namely that the world *is* as the work shows it to be'. For, 'the mediums of art enable works of art to show or present states of affairs to contemplation, states of affairs which may suggest but which do not assert further states beyond the world of the work' (Diffey 1995: 210).

have left aside literary appreciation and stepped into something more like social science or philosophy: we are now asking questions about the world and not the work. Literary texts paradigmatically present fictional narratives, stories about characters and events that are not, and these are the objects before us when appreciating the work as a work of literary fiction. We may reflect or hypothesize and ask whether the world is like that of the text, or what it would be like if it were. But these are questions the world answers, not the text. Thus, the sceptic argues, worldly questions, moral and cognitive insights as the indirect humanist conceives them, have no relevance to a theory of literature and literary value. They are two independent activities, the literary theorist's and the humanist's: the literary theorist wants to understand the text better, the humanist wants to turn from the text to see what the world has to say about the visions presented in it.

This is not always appreciated as it should be. One finds much ink spilt in recent aesthetics on how works of literature might help improve our faculty of imagination, develop our cognitive skills, discover what we would think, feel, or value if in another's shoes, become more sympathetic and adept moral reasoners, and so on.[14] These are genuine cognitive achievements, and literature can certainly help us in our pursuit of them. But claims of this sort tend to say too much about readers and too little about literary works. Since literary works are, for obvious reasons, rarely *about* the imagination, cognitive skills, or emotions of their readers, to gesture towards these things in an attempt to defend humanism is to gesture towards very much the wrong thing. The question is primarily textual: it concerns the nature of the literary, of what we find of worldly significance when we look *inside* a literary work. It is only about readers—about the ways in which their minds and morals can be improved through their encounters with literature—in a secondary, derivative sense.

---

[14] See Novitz (1987); Nussbaum (1995); Walton (in Hjort and Laver 1997); and Harold (2003) for examples of such views.

To see this, consider a classics student who, having been asked to read Plato's *Symposium*, returns to his teacher and claims to have learnt much from it. The teacher asks the student to explain exactly what he has learnt, to which he replies, 'a considerable amount of Attic Greek and some fine metaphors for drunkenness'. He very well may have learnt this—one can find all this in Plato's dialogue—and he might be all the better for it. But naturally the teacher will think that the student has missed the point of the assignment. The student has learnt something, but he has not learnt it from Plato. This is because what he claims to have learnt makes no reference at all to what we might describe as the *cognitive labour* of Plato's dialogue, to the lesson *it* wishes to impart, to the insight *it* struggles to articulate—assuming as I am that Plato intends in that dialogue to illuminate the nature of love and not the grammar of Attic Greek or our capacity to speak in metaphors.

Likewise, any attempt to defend humanism that puts all the emphasis on how readers might become more successful moral agents, emoters, and reasoners is in the end simply a more sophisticated example of the mistake of the classics student. It is valuable to have accounts of how engagements with the literary affect readers in morally and intellectually positive ways. We do live in a culture in which art is at times thought to be of no more significance than its ability to amuse, and these accounts do much to counter literary philistinism of this brand. But as a response to the question of whether literary works themselves are or can be revelatory of reality, they are not very satisfying. In fact, they are largely silent on the matter.

Though the sceptic's argument is directed against a specific way of explaining the connection between literature and reality, it should be easy to see how he can develop it in ways that will infect any picture of humanism that casts the relation between text and world as indirect. The indirect humanist accepts that there is a divide between reality and literature, and he tries to bring the two closer through the activities of imagination, reflection, simulation, and so forth. This makes the sceptic's job very easy, *for as long as there is a divide, the* sceptic can always point to it and show that the humanist is standing on the wrong side of it, the side of the world and not the literary work.[15] It does not matter how closely the humanist draws together the two sides of the divide, for, as long as there is a divide, the sceptic can show that whatever bridge the humanist attempts to construct will always lead from what is in the literary text to what is outside it, and thus to what lies outside the purview of genuine literary-textual understanding. The sceptic can show, in short, that the humanist is always a step too far from the literary work.

We now have an idea of why literary humanists, as odd as it might sound on first hearing, have often been thought to be anti-literary, prone to lose literature in the very attempt to capture its value. It is fine to speak of what use we can make of a literary work, of its instrumental value in pursuing other goals (such as grasping human relations with the complexity and understanding Austin, Dostoevsky, or Melville do in their novels). But, if we try to develop this into a full-blooded theory of literary humanism, the sceptic has no trouble cutting the humanist's lifeline and letting the world float away in the name of literature. The sceptic does not attack our humanist intuition because he is an anti-literary brute. On the contrary, he voices a concern that is reasonable and genuinely respectful of the literary. He fights against what he sees as vulgar strain in speaking about the value of literature, one of relegating its status to that of serving non-literary interests; he refuses to let us

---

[15] It is for these reasons that I find Martha Nussbaum as unhelpful for the development of the humanist intuition as I find her interesting, and this explains why I say so little about this important philosopher. Consider this passage: 'Imagination is the chief instrument of the good. It is more or less a commonplace to say that a person's ideas and treatment of his fellows are dependent upon his power to put himself imaginatively in their place... Wherever social divisions and barriers exist, practices and ideas that correspond to them fix metes and bounds, so that liberal action is placed under restraint... Art is a mode of prediction not found in charts and statistics, and it insinuates possibilities of human relations not to be found in rule and precept, admonition and administration' (Nussbaum 1995: 348). Her theory is more complex than is expressed in this passage, but the reliance on possibility and imagination we find in her works seems to me always to invite the arguments against indirect humanism I am giving here.

explain our connection to literature in terms of its ability to promote extra-literary pursuits, in terms of those personal and social activities that may be improved if we adopt the perspective given expression in a work of literature. It may be part and parcel of taking *Middlemarch* seriously as a literary text that I think from within its perspective, grasping the moral complexity of the world presented by that work. It is another thing altogether to express its value in terms of how I might become a smarter, nicer person by coming to regard real-life situations with this same perspective.

If we recall the old joke about the tennis player who tells his lover that what he likes best about their romantic life is that it improves his on-court stamina, we might say that the sceptic, like the slighted lover, thinks that the significance of the activity at hand has been ignored. What the sceptic rightly requires is that the humanist cast his theory in terms of actual features of literary content. And *this* is what he claims the indirect humanist is unable to do. The sceptic is not a formalist or subscriber to that unlovable position called 'aestheticism'. He has no interest in showing that the only acceptable ways to encounter the literary work of art consist in attending to merely linguistic, purely technical, or solely structural features of work. The sceptic requires only that an account of what we value in a literary work specify a value a literary work actually puts on offer, and leaves the humanist free to characterize this value as he wishes—aesthetic, ethical, formal, cognitive—as long as he can meet this basic condition (standards of reasonableness notwithstanding). The sceptic's arguments function to stop humanists looking outside the text when searching for its value, as they often do, and he is very reasonable to demand this.

The scepetic's arguments bring to view a constraint on what can count as a response to the problem of literary humanism. We might call it the 'textual constraint' and treat it as telling us that a satisfactory account of a proper feature of a literary work requires that whatever property we attribute to a text—say the property of being revelatory of reality—be an actual property *of* the text: something we come into contact with when we explore the interior of the work. It must be a part of its *content*, broadly construed. So, if a certain point about or insight into reality is not *in* the work, then, according to this textual constraint, we cannot invoke that point or insight when trying to locate a bridge that leads from the work to reality. The important question from the literary standpoint is what we find when we look within a literary work. And, if it is something not quite in the work, then that something cannot be invoked to explain a value, power, or accomplishment of that work. If we fail to respect this, we are ignoring the literary work, much as the student of Plato ignored Plato. We are merely commenting on how we can enlist the text in our personal intellectual pursuits and ultimately saying nothing about how the literary work of art itself can be revelatory of reality.

1.2. THE SCEPTIC'S RECITAL

We are beginning to see how important it was to include the idea of directness in the initial description of the humanism. We will now see how problematic it is. The upshot of the argument of 1.1 is that the humanist fails to say something that illuminates the nature of literature if he tries to develop his intuition by casting it as an indirect relation between work and world, describing it as an act of carrying over what we see in the literary text to what lies outside it. And this forces us to see how important it is to find a way of describing the world as in some sense an internal textual property, something we encounter *in* the text. But the sceptic has a number of arguments that suggest that taking the step from an indirect humanism to a direct humanism is impossible.

There is not *an* argument against the idea that we can have a direct vision of our world in a work of literature. There are rather a number of observations, all sharing in common a very entrenched idea of how world-directed uses of language function, making the idea of direct humanism look like either hyperbole or idiocy: at best an overemphasizing of the fact that literary texts borrow bits and pieces of our world when constructing their narratives; at worst a failure to grasp the elementary distinction between fictional worlds and the real one.

As Lubomír Doležel puts it, implicit in the distinction between literary fiction and non-fictional writing is a contrast between 'world-constructing' and 'world-imaging' texts and discourse forms, in effect a distinction between texts that attempt to describe the world and those that attempt to create one.[16] Literary texts are not empirically adequate statements of fact. Indeed, they seem to be not at all interested in engaging in a form of—to use Stephen Davies's apt phrase—'informational discourse'.[17] It is built into our idea of 'reading something as literary fiction' that we do not take the text to be constrained, like a journalist's report, by the facts; it is built into our understanding of its sentences that they are in this sense 'beyond truth-valuation'.[18] And this implies an independence of literary content from factual content; indeed, it suggests that the presence of the former reveals a turning-away from the latter. World-imaging texts are built out of an attempt to offer factual content. For this reason we can speak of their descriptions and statements as running by way of world, praising them on these grounds when they succeed and criticizing them on these grounds when they fail (such as when we criticize an inaccurate history text). There is, we can already see, no obvious role for these conditions and constraints to play in our theoretical understanding of a textual form such as literary fiction. It is at root world-constructing, and thus the sceptic claims that we have no clear idea of what it might even mean to say that its words attempt to offer up a view of the our-worldly.

For the sceptic this brings to view a key point: literary language does not use the basic semantic–linguistic tools that account for the possibility of connecting words to world. Literature is not brought before the basic semantic court of worldly truth and reference. It is not an account of actual states of affairs and so we lose at the gate the

---

[16] Doležel (1998: 24).   [17] Davies (2006: 216).   [18] Doležel (1998: 24).

idea that the words of literature function to refer to or make truth claims about reality. But without these semantic tools for bridging word and world, we appear to have no way of developing the claim that literature offers up reality directly in the presentation of literary content.[19]

If literary texts functioned to provide a genuine view of reality, at the very least we would have to find grounds for claiming that the descriptions found in them are guided and constrained by what happens in the real world. In ordinary speech, what connects my statement 'my landlord is trying to evict me' to reality is the fact that my landlord is (actually, really, and so on.) trying to evict me. In short, the connection lies in the fact that my words represent his actions. Otherwise my words are empty of world: either a lie or, if woven into a narrative line, a candidate for a work of fiction—but in neither case informative of how things stand in reality. Most of the statements we find in a literary text turn out to be strictly false when applied to the actual world: that Poseidon 'remained angry with the godlike Odysseus' is not true of anyone in the real world. And this is no surprise, since it does not refer to anyone in the real world. It 'refers' to Odysseus of Homer's *Odyssey*.[20] It represents nothing real, and that we do not thereby take the claim to be false—that we do not dismiss its content as misinformed or just wrong— brings home the fact that questions of worldly truth and reference are largely irrelevant when evaluating the content of a novel.

With only slight exaggeration, the sceptic can put it this way: *literary texts describe their own creations*. In the very act of describing the happenings of the story, in the very act of creating literary content, literary texts generate the characters and events to which

---

[19] Properly speaking, truth is a semantic value, while reference, representation, and correspondence are semantic relations. I use 'semantic tools' or 'semantic devices' as an umbrella term to cover both these core types of semantic values and 'semantic relations' to describe the most general ways in which sentential content can be said to be *about* the world (by referring to it, etc.).

[20] I use 'refer' in scare quotes because it is questionable whether we should say that the description of, for example, Odysseus in the poem *refers* to this character (if we think that reference requires an actual object we run into obvious trouble).

their descriptions refer. The descriptions and representations we find in literary texts are 'representations' of constructs of language. Othello, at least the character found in Shakespeare's *Othello*, does not exist outside the text. So, when the words of that text describe Othello, they do not reach beyond the text to any particular bit of reality. In this sense a work of literary fiction creates its own history, one that is expressly not, as fiction, the history of the real world. As Stanley Cavell says, with typical Cavellean bombast, literature has 'the power to stipulate the world from beginning to end'.[21]

We should notice that none of the sceptic's arguments proposes the patently absurd idea that works of imaginative literature speak exclusively about the imaginary and the unreal, a claim that would imply that, when William Faulkner wrote *As I Lay Dying*, he invented not only Addie Bundren but also Mississippi, wagons, and death. Literary texts as a matter of course use features of our world in the construction of their narratives.[22] The real world and its history often provide settings for the literary; they provide a backdrop for the action (praxis) of the narrative line. But literary texts do not refer to or make truth claims about this backdrop of reality; *they use it*. Of course we do criticize a novel that uses New York as its background setting yet fails to get straight the difference between Downtown and Uptown. But this is a critique of the setting's accuracy, and it is done along the lines in which we criticize a set in a play rather than an argument to the effect that the text attempts to make truth claims

---

[21] Cavell (1979: 457).
[22] Norman Mailer's *The Executioner's Song* is one of the most often cited examples of this, a novel whose narrative line follows in nearly all its detail an actual event. Yet we find in this text, as with other historical dramas and so-called New Journalist writing, layers of imaginative invention added to the (real) events upon which the story is built. Even in cases of what is often called *metalepsis*—this blurring of the boundary between fact and fiction—we find a tremendous amount of information the nature of which makes it impossible to treat the text as in any way straightforwardly representational. As soon as we find a fictionalizing embellishment in a seemingly empirically based text (characteristically descriptions of a character's thoughts or transcriptions of historical conversations, presented not as hypotheses but as direct reports—to which the author could never be privy), we begin to see that we have lost the grounds for treating it as a genuine world-imaging text (for the reasons I give above).

about the world and fails in so doing. Saying so much—claiming that accuracy of background setting is straightforwardly truth-functional or referential—would be akin to saying that the set in a production of *A Street Car Named Desire* functions to make truth claims about New Orleans, which is obvious nonsense. Thus the sceptic points out that the backdrops and settings we find in literature, just as with stage sets, are accurate or inaccurate, not true or false. They are used, well or badly; they are not asserted of the world, truly or falsely.[23]

The sceptic can provide a simple example to bring his point home. If we discovered that everything described in *Othello* transpired in the real world, we would not thereby say that its assertions were made *of* the world. The reason for this is simple: the assertions are made of Shakespeare's *Othello*. It is because Iago says in Shakespeare's work 'I follow him to serve my turn upon him' that we are entitled to claim that Iago is bent on revenge, regardless of what happens in any real-world playing-out of Shakespeare's tragedy. To say otherwise is to fail to grasp that claims about what happens in a literary text are justified only by reference to what is said in that text: no glimpse into empirical history plays any role in determining whether we can really say Iago is bent on revenge in *Othello*. For we would never—and this is built into our idea of reading something as a work of imaginative literature—claim that it is *false* that Shakespeare's Iago is bent on revenge if the play failed to match empirical history at this point alone.

As we have seen (and as we already knew), reality does not bestow upon a literary work the right to speak about its characters and events as it so chooses (as we would say that it is because Caesar was murdered that a historian has the right to make this claim). We might say that Shakespeare is a prophet, or a thief, if we find that his writings match history word for word; but we would not say that we have found grounds for claiming that literary language can

[23] As Lamarque and Olsen argue, we explain the presence of empirically adequate statements by invoking not worldly reference but 'the category of fictional content subject to the fictive stance, that is, content of a factual nature presented in the fictive mode and integrated into a wider fictional context' (Lamarque and Olsen 1994: 66)

be seen as retaining the standard semantic functions of non-literary uses of language simply because it contains descriptions that turn out to be empirically adequate. Even in those cases where we find statements that can also be applied correctly to the world (and they are characteristically few and trivial: there would be nothing interesting in a humanism that supported itself on the sundry world-adequate historical and geographical descriptions found in a text), the sceptic points out that in literary works they are used to state 'facts' about the narrative line, serving to illuminate it rather than what lies beyond it. One often cites Italo Calvino here, as he reminds us of this when he begins his famous novel with the following request: 'You are about to begin reading Italo Calvino's new novel, *If on a Winter's Night a Traveller*. Relax. Concentrate. Dispel every other thought. Let the world around you fade.'

Superficial points of contact between the world of the reader and the world of the literary work will hold, of course. 'Hat' in a literary work still means *hat* and 'pain' still means *pain*, at least until a work indicates otherwise. The sceptic is not a fool. He does not remove literature so far from reality that he destroys this obvious condition of its intelligibility. He accounts for this by pointing out that literary texts retain the sense of our terms, and thus the words and descriptions we find in world-constructing texts retain their standard meanings. The system we often find in bookstores of placing books into 'literature' and 'non-fiction' sections turns out to be done along the lines of Frege's distinction between sense and reference. Literature and world-directed texts share the same language, generally put.[24] They both participate in the same *Sinn*. But literary language stays on the level of *Sinn*, whereas, in standard

---

[24] The following characterization of Frege is fairly common in literary theory. It has its roots in the following observation in *On Sense and Reference*: 'In hearing an epic poem we are... interested only in the sense of the sentences and the images and feelings thereby aroused. The question of truth would cause us to abandon aesthetic delight for the attitude of scientific investigation. Hence it is a matter of no concern for us whether the name "Odysseus" has reference, so long as we accept the poem as a work of art' (Frege 1970: 63). It is often argued that the independence of sense and reference implied here does not square well with Frege's general philosophy (it is common to claim that in

(empirical) use, language takes the extra step of applying these words to the actual world. And, if we cast it this way, the sceptic shows that this commonality of meaning, this sharing of mere sense, does nothing to bring literature into significant contact with our world. Literature, we might say, begins the race with all other forms of writing; it stands along with them on the line of meaningful speech. It is that just literature stays there, whereas other forms of writing go forward to apply words to reality, to make the leap to worldly reference and hence world-directed speech.[25]

The sceptic leaves us with the following picture: since worldly truth, reference, and (more generally) representation do not guide—indeed are absent from—the literary use of language, literature cannot present to us a direct vision of reality. It is because of the semantic functions of language, because language gets beyond itself as it were and latches onto something external to it, that it is not hopelessly self-referential. Indeed, it is because of this system of reference, of (to cast the net wider) mirroring and imaging the actual, that words can aspire to be revelatory of something called reality, that they can aspire to cast light on the world of the speaker. The sceptic shows that literary language performs none of these semantic acts, and thus that humanism, requiring as it does that literary language be revelatory of our world, appears a hopeless position. The humanist asks us to accept that literature informs us about our world when the very nature of literary language—its wedding words to fictions—makes it tremendously difficult to find anything that is real enough in a literary text to ground a humanist view of literature.

The sceptic's argument against the idea that we can have a direct vision of reality in a literary work remains strong even if we weaken

Fregean semantics there can be no sense without reference), but this is another concern, one that will take us too far afield to explore here.

[25] For better or worse, depending on one's bent. This idea might underlie the anti-literary argument that literature is trivial. It also underlies many of the structuralist and poststructuralist notions that in literature language examines itself, drawing attention to the word itself rather than to what the word signifies (think, if you want, of the idea that poetry functions not to describe extra-textual reality but to bring into view the aesthetic features of language).

its central claim: that literature speaks about fictions rather than about how things stand in our world. We might accept, if just for the sake of argument, that literary works, though largely composed of fictional content, can engage in straightforward, 'world-directed', psychological, political, theological (and so on) commentary; that writers of imaginative fiction, when so inclined, can speak about the world just as philosophers, historians, and journalists do. We can accept all this. But it is of no use in developing an account of humanism, and the reasons for this should now be clear. It is because the idea of humanism requires that we look at literature *just* when it strikes us as fictional. We are asking whether works of *fiction* can act as a window on the world, and this requires not finding a level of non-fictional discourse in works of literature but finding a way to reconcile the fictional and the real. It calls on us to explain how the frame of fiction can function to open up a view of the real. This is what the sceptic denies the humanist can show.

For this reason it is not enough to try to respond to the sceptic by asking whether it is possible that there be a text—*any*—that blurs the boundary between fictional and non-fictional forms of writing. Surely there are many, but finding examples of them will not help us. The question that humanism hangs on is a very precise one, one that concerns our *actual* literary heritage, specifically all those works within it that are content to speak about fictions. These are what we are trying to make sense of. We are asking why we give such status to—why we take so *seriously*—Medea's madness, Othello's jealousy, Baldwin's depiction of a lynching (a fictional lynching, but, for all that, a horrible fiction). There would be little to recommend a theory that rested on the claim that a humanistic stance can be assumed only in those cases where we find *something other than fiction* in works of fiction. In fact, it would amount to an avoidance of the question itself.

We might consider a not uncommon experience when teaching and attending conferences on aesthetics, that of the student or colleague who claims to have solved the problem by pointing out that certain well-known science-fiction serials speak (directly, perhaps truthfully) about the possibility of time travel, the difference between minds in humans and 'minds' in machines, even the feasibility of communication with a cosmic Other. Perhaps they do, but—one always wants to say—so what? For, unless one wants to offer a response that gives, say, a *Star Trek* novel pride of place among those works of fiction that can be read for life and no place at all to Shakespeare's tragedies, Faulkner's novels, Nabokov's satires, responses of this sort will prove to be thoroughly unhelpful. This might strike one as a deliberately ridiculous example. But it is worth noting that any attempt to give support to humanism by finding a layer of non-fiction in works of literary fiction will be every bit as silly, and for quite the same reasons.[26]

1.3. LITERARY ISOLATIONISM

As I said earlier, it is wrong to think that the sceptic is an anti-literary brute. He begins his recital not as a spoilsport (as perhaps the logical positivists did when it came to aesthetics), simply denying that texts have something significant to say to us about ourselves and asking that we turn our attention to more serious affairs. He wants, and for reasons that are respectable, to remind us that we should treat a literary work as an object of appreciation in its own right. And he sees his arguments as giving necessity to these claims. He sees the

---

[26] I have omitted a discussion of ways some older versions of literary humanism have grappled with this—namely, by arguing that literature can be seen as describing reality by referring to or representing *universals and types*, making claims about the world in this sense. Humanists of this stripe often argue from the claim that fictions are mimeses of general properties (say 'jealousy')—universals in this sense—to the conclusion that they somehow function to refer to or speak assertively (and so informatively) about these universals. But this clearly will not work. A mimetic relation specifies the extent to which one thing resembles some other thing; a referential relation specifies how descriptions function to make claims about something, and one cannot siphon a referential relation from a merely mimetic one. From Anna Karenina's mimetic success, from the fact that she speaks and behaves so much like a *type* of person—say (for convenience) the Suffering Lover—we may well find in the real world, we cannot argue that her lifelike-ness *is* asserting or saying something about this type.

upshot of his scepticism about literary humanism as showing us that we must turn our attention from what the literary text does not and cannot touch (reality) and direct it towards its proper object: the work itself. It is not that the sceptic wants to take away the humanist's desire to find genuine value in literature. He rather wants to correct what he sees as the traditional humanist desire to locate value always in insights into reality (the sceptic might be seen as asking us to see literature as offering an alternative realm of value, and so expanding value in this sense, rather than trying to fit it always into the same box: worldly understanding). He wants to prevent us from trying to make literature a window to the world—and thus something we do not properly look *at* but *through*—instead of a free-standing source of its own value.

Though it would be impossible here to offer a full account of the different ways contemporary philosophers and theorists of literature implicitly express this scepticism in offering their accounts of literature, we might speak fairly of 'drifts', and characterize the two drifts dominant (in Anglo-American universities and scholarship at least) as the 'poststructuralist drift'[27] and the 'analytic drift'. Philosophers and critics such as Roland Barthes, Paul de Man, and, most notably, Jacques Derrida undeniably float along the poststructuralist,[28] while philosophers such as Kendall Walton, John Searle, Peter Lamarque, and Gregory Currie float calmly along the

---

[27] It may be true that poststructuralism's (and more specifically deconstructivism's) star is fading in current literary theory, giving way to cultural theory and the like. But the effect of poststructural thinking on theories of meaning and language—its profound relativism and anti-realism—is still pervasive in literary studies, and a discussion of it brings to view a way of thinking about literature that finds expression in a great swath of current work in literary and cultural studies. To give a sense of how sanctified the classic arguments of deconstruction are still taken to be, in a recent book on poststructuralism a prominent literary theorist wrote, apparently without irony: 'And yet *Of Grammatology* delivered a resounding challenge to the entire tradition of Western philosophy, and although the book has been endlessly misread, it arguments have not so far been effectively refuted' (Belsey 2002: 74).

[28] At least this can be said of Barthes by the time he wrote *S/Z* (1974), which is often taken to mark his transition from structuralism to poststructuralism. For the classic works of these poststructuralist authors, see also Derrida (1978) and de Man (1979).

analytic (philosophers such as Richard Rorty and Umberto Eco might be seen as having a foot in both, though clearly starting out in different drifts themselves). There is often a tremendous antagonism between the two drifts, exemplified wonderfully in the famous debate between Derrida and Searle,[29] which resulted, depending on who you talk to, as revealing either the inherent nonsense of poststructuralist thought or the naive and nearly puritanical confines of contemporary analytical philosophy. I would agree with philosophers such as Richard Rorty who claim that this animosity inclines towards exaggeration and is usually misplaced, often boiling down to not much more than a tendency to criticize a theorist because she fails to speak in the vocabulary of a traditional Anglo-American philosopher or a French literary critic (depending on the drift from within which one is doing the criticizing). At any rate, here I have little interest in the antagonism or arguing for one drift over the other. Indeed, what I want to draw attention to in this section is that, at least from the vantage point of the humanist, they look much more like allies than is often noticed.

Perhaps the best way to bring the basics of the poststructuralist drift into view is to explain what it is a reaction to: structuralist linguistics and criticism (in particular that of Saussure).[30] Structuralists argued that meaning is not immanent in a sign or linguistic unit but is rather a product of the relations of different units to one another. The word 'tree' has meaning, for example, not because it bears some intrinsic or natural correlation with the extra-linguistic items with which we are all familiar. Meaning is made possible only within the structure of a language, a function of the way in which the system relates linguistic items to one another and in so doing marks the roles they play in a language. Meaning is made possible by these differential relations

---

[29] See Derrida (1977) and Searle (1977).
[30] Most notably Saussure (1974). It may be an overstatement to say—nowadays at least—that poststructuralism is a reaction to structuralism, though it certainly grew into a movement as a reaction to structuralism and is fruitfully understood in this light (as Wittgenstein's later philosophy is well described as a reaction to his own earlier writings and those of Russell and Frege).

rather than through the establishment of isolated matches between words and items in the world (hence the Structuralist dictum that meaning is 'relational' and not 'substantial'). As Structuralists often said: *meaning is difference*, a function of a system of differentiation.

This picture of meaning as relational is the first pillar of structuralist accounts of meaning. The second pillar is the so-called unity of signifier and signified. In virtue of this stable structure of 'difference', the items within the system, words or signifiers, can be related to signifieds, the concepts expressed by words. We take the relations of words, of signifiers understood as marks and noises, and relate them to 'signifieds'. And this unity of signifier and signified in turn blows sense into the sounds we make and scribbles we write, producing the basic unit of communication: the 'sign' ('tree' as a linguistic vehicle for expressing the concept Tree). The structure of the language can change and shift as much as it wants: as long as it provides a stable differentiation of signs, it can account for the determinacy of meaning, for a sturdy system of relations between signifiers and signifieds.

The most convenient way to characterize the diverse bodies of work that make up the poststructuralist drift is to say that the poststructuralist accepts the first pillar of structuralism but rejects the second: language *is* difference but there is no firm or fixed relationship between signifier and signified and so no genuine stability of meaning.[31] It is often hard to find an argument for this, in the sense of some unified or generally accepted way of stating why signifiers never fully yield a signified. And this, I am inclined to think, is largely

---

[31] Umberto Eco (1994) draws attention to Derrida's dependence on a particular argument given by C. S. Peirce. I quote Peirce's argument here, if only because one might find it helpful to see my above gloss of the poststructuralist drift expressed in a more familiar vocabulary (if we replace 'representation' with 'signifier' and 'sign' in obvious places the point of comparison should be clear): 'The meaning of a representation can be nothing but a representation. In fact it is nothing but the representation itself conceived as stripped of irrelevant clothing. But this clothing can never be completely stripped off: it is only changed for something more diaphanous. So there is an infinite regression here. Finally the interpretant is nothing but another representation, it has its interpretant again. Lo, another infinite series' (Peirce 1969: 32).

because many poststructuralists accomplish this severing of signifier and signified in the act of analysing specific texts, generalizing their claims based on their critical discoveries (poststructuralism, at least in the English-speaking world, is most popular as a literary-theoretical rather than philosophical movement).[32]

Nevertheless, we can get at the basic poststructuralist insight as follows. We saw that for the structuralist the correlation between signifier and signified is expressed in the sign, and that the determinacy of the sign (what makes it *this* sign) is a product of the differential relations of all the signs in the language. And we might see a tension here. Nothing outside the relation between signs fixes the meaning of a sign. This much is implied by the structuralist view of meaning; and the poststructuralist argues that a system of difference between signs is just not the sort of thing that can secure determinacy of meaning. There turns out to be no way of limiting the relations that constitute the meaning of a sign and so no way of fully capturing the meaning of a sign. If the specification of what makes a sign *this* sign is a matter of its relations to the other signs in the language, so must be the specification of its meaning. So, to account for the determinacy of a sign, we have to trace all the differential relations of that sign. But this search soon shows itself to be endless. There is no moment at which I come to an end of the process of difference. I am only put in contact with more signs, each calling for others to mark their (putative) determinacy.[33] I am never put in touch with a sort of last-word in this structure that

---

[32] Rorty offers a succinct explanation of why we seem to find so little of what the analytic-minded philosopher would consider to be proper arguments for this: 'When philosophers such as Derrida say things like "there is nothing outside the text" they are not making theoretical remarks, remarks backed up by epistemological or semantical arguments... They are not claiming to have discovered the *real* nature of truth, language or literature. Rather, they are saying that the very notion of discovering the *nature* of such things is part of the intellectual framework which we must abandon—part of what Heidegger calls "the metaphysics of presence" or "the onto-theological tradition"' (Rorty 1982: 140).

[33] It is often pointed out how much this has in common with certain mainstays of analytical philosophy since the 1950s, including scepticism about rule following but in particular Quine's thesis of the indeterminacy of translation (and the literature on

expresses the determinacy of a sign. And, if a conclusive specification of meaning cannot be had, we are no longer entitled to claim that we can close our hands around a determinate sign and thus over a final, properly circumscribed meaning. The process of locating a determinate meaning is interminable; meaning is always 'deferred', taking a step back with every step we take towards it. Umberto Eco puts the upshot of all this nicely when he writes: 'Since the process foresees the unlimited shifting from symbol to symbol, the meaning of a text is always postponed. The only meaning of a text is "I mean more". But since that "more" will be interpreted by a further "I mean more", the final meaning of text is an empty secret'.[34]

We should also mention Derrida's occult but immensely influential claim that:

If reading must not be content with doubling the text, it cannot legitimately transgress the text toward something other than it, towards a referent (a reality that is metaphysical, historical, psychobiographical, etc.) or toward a signified object outside the text whose content could take place, could have taken place, outside language... There is no outside the text (*il n'y a pas de hors-texte*).[35]

There is an obvious reason we do not often hear of poststructural (or deconstructive) humanists. It is very hard to see how something about our world can be proposed, established, revealed, or shown in a text that does not, by its very nature, make determinate claims at

---

interpretation that follows in its vein). For an accessible discussion of this see Putnam (1983).

[34] Umberto Eco (1990: 27). Eco is careful to state that instability of meaning does not imply a kind of 'anything goes' theory of interpretation, which many (usually uninformed) philosophers fear poststructuralism endorses (though arguably in the hands of less philosophically talented literary critics it is often used this way). As Eco puts it: 'But, even though the interpreters cannot decide which interpretation is the privileged [interpretation], they can agree on the fact that certain interpretations are not contextually legitimated. Thus, even though using a text as a playground for implementing unlimited semiosis, they can agree that at certain moments the "play of musement" can transitorily stop by producing a consensual judgment. Indeed, symbols grow but do not remain empty' (Eco 1994: 42).

[35] Derrida (1976: 158).

all.[36] If the sceptic argues against humanism by showing that *literary* language has no extra-textual reference, the poststructuralist takes the sceptic's argument a step further: *language* does not connect us to the extra-linguistic, for in severing the signifier from the signified we lose our point of contact. In this respect the poststructuralist might be seen as simply extending the sceptic's view of literature to the whole of language itself. And the resultant 'deferral' of meaning only makes things worse for our humanist intuition. We cannot tame a text's semantic spasms enough to make it a spokesperson for something outside of it, since we cannot find within it anything resembling a voice sufficiently constant and unified to be capable of such a thing. We do not have a direct vision of anything extra-textual. What we find is the free play of meaning, and, for the poststructuralist, reading and in particular criticism become a sort of communion with the very nature of the language, an opportunity to examine and behold the vacillation of meaning and so the steady proliferation of interpretative possibilities. The poststructuralist exchanges the humanist's desire to find a vision of world for what she takes to be an honest view of the instability of language.

When we turn to the analytic drift we tend to see, to continue with poststructuralist vocabulary, not a wholesale claim to the effect that there is nothing outside the text[37]—with all its anti-realist implications—but a picture of literature that suggests that whatever is outside the *literary* text is beyond the reach of the words of that text. Much of the analytic drift of literary theory is continuous with the general analytic interest in the nature of truth, reference, and correspondence (or, rather, grows out of this. I discuss this in detail in Chapter 5). I doubt it would be much of an overstatement to say that the current analytic drift in the philosophy of literature grew

---

[36] Except, of course, the instability of language, which one might argue is a kind of showing. See Harrison (1991) for a very interesting attempt to reconcile humanism and deconstruction.

[37] Whatever this might precisely mean. Rorty has been attacked for treating it as the claim that there are nothing but texts, the so-called thesis of strong textualism.

out of the desire to find an adequate way to make sense of sentences and descriptions that are not false (like lies) yet are not true in any straightforward sense: in short the problem of fiction. Much of the work we find in the beginnings of this drift, from Macdonald, Isenberg, and Beardsley[38] onwards, has the shape it does because of the way in which theorists wrestled with this problem. What we see in this drift is a palpable preoccupation with the philosophical and linguistic problems raised by the element of fictionality in literature; and the overriding interest becomes one of showing that, while we do not take literary texts' descriptions to be fact, we nevertheless do not, as Russell once appeared content to claim, read them as a continuous string of simply *false* claims.[39]

We might divide the popular contemporary approaches in the analytic drift into the 'modal' and 'imaginative' theories. The modal and imaginative strains are not competing schools in the analytic drift; and I should make clear that this is a distinction of convenience—I am trying to characterize a considerable mass of theories here—rather than an account of incompatible general outlooks (philosophers of both strains can, and do, borrow freely from one another). Modal theories tend to speak of fictional worlds as special classes of *possible* worlds.[40] It is a method that was given its best-known philosophical formulation by David Lewis; and literary theorists such as Lubomír Doležel, Thomas Pavel, and Umberto Eco (at least his foray into his 'small-worlds' theory) have worked it into vigorous theories of literary–fictive understanding.[41] The problem of fiction in literature here becomes somewhat like the problem of counterfactuals in the

---

[38] See Isenberg (1954–5), MacDonald (1954), and Beardsley (1981).
[39] Russell (1962: 277).
[40] Typically as *incomplete* possible worlds, since 'only some conceivable statements about fictional entities are decidable' (Doležel 1998: 22). As the argument often goes: with a genuine possible world there are in principle grounds for determining the truth value of every statement we can make about it. This condition does not hold in fictional possible worlds, since there is nothing to establish the truth of claims such as 'Othello's great-grandfather was a sailor' or (following the common example) 'Sherlock Homes had X number of hairs on his head'; the texts are indeterminate in respect of the truth values of these sentences, and many others.
[41] See Lewis (1978); Pavel (1986); Eco (1994); and Doležel (1998).

philosophy of language, one of describing the mechanism that allows a writer to *describe* actions and events that never actually occurred (or allows a reader to understand and appreciate statements made about them: how we are able to make truth-valued and referential statements about non-actual states of affairs, for example).

The imaginative theorists, on the other hand, tend to emphasize the type of *attitude* that is invited by the work of fiction. Walton's ingenious 'mimesis as make-believe' theory is the best known and most influential. Here it is argued that, just as children use sticks and stones as swords and bombs in a game of make-believe, when adults read literature they use words in much the same way. We do not *believe* what we read in *Othello*, since we cannot believe a sentence (or a text composed of sentences) we know is not true. But we can *make-believe* them, and so we treat Shakespeare's descriptions in *Othello* as props for our imaginative involvement in the storyline. Very few philosophers except Walton himself are happy to use the term 'game' to describe this (for one thing it hints that literary involvement is less than properly serious); but it is impossible to overstate how widespread the use of the notion of make-believe is (and cognate attitudes) in the contemporary analytic drift. What the imaginative theorists have in common is the starting point of accepting that texts assert nothing about how things stand in the world—they have neither worldly truth nor reference. But they recognize that, if we stopped there, literature, and particularly the role it plays in a culture, would be utterly mysterious. The imaginative theorist tries to bring literary fiction back to us as a respectable, autonomous cultural practice; and she does this by investigating the ability of non-epistemic attitudes to ground the possibility of entering into a fictional world and appreciating it as *something* though we know all the while that it is really nothing at all.

It would be false to say that philosophers of the analytic drift are anti-humanists. In fact, I would imagine most would take umbrage at such a claim. But, as we might have already noticed, this drift shares in common with the sceptic the picture of literary content as presenting to view something essentially otherworldly—at least not *our-worldly*, and so at first glance it is not a particularly inviting position for the humanist. As usually developed, it seems at best compatible with a theory of indirect humanism and so no viable form of humanism at all. The sceptical position I have developed is essentially a way of drawing out the implications of the claim that functions as a starting point in the analytic drift: the descriptions found in literature are not asserted of the world. Our sceptic simply turns his attention to the implications this carries for the idea of humanism, how far this takes the literary from the our-worldly. If the first thing we have to say about our involvement in literary fiction is that (following the modal theorist) it concerns possible worlds, or (following the imaginative theorist) it subsumes the world of the text into an object of make-believe, then the idea of seeing reality *in* a literary text is made mysterious. The idea that literature is otherworldly seems built into the basic vocabulary of the analytic drift. It tells us that novels offer us either make-believed worlds or worlds that are possible and so not quite our own.[42] Although there may not be the antagonism to the humanist intuition that we often find in the poststructuralist drift, the idea of a *direct* vision of reality is rendered senseless. If we set up the problem as philosophers of the analytic drift do, we immediately invite the sceptic's recital, for all the sceptic's arguments flow from the way in which the world–word relation is cast in the analytic drift. The analytic drift *begins* with the notion that the normal semantic functions of language are lacking in literature, and the sceptic merely taps the humanist on the shoulder and points out what this implies.

There is one important respect in which we can see a shared picture in the poststructuralist and analytic drifts, one that shows them, at least in the eyes of the humanist, to have the same water running under them. Eric Miller puts the nature of the assumption in these terms:

---

[42] Or whatever combination of *possibilia* and *imaginatio* one might build into one's theory: modal and imaginative theories need not be seen as mutually exclusive positions, since a possible world can be treated as an imagined world, and so forth.

From such a foundational commitment to reference and correspondence-truth flows the rest of the scientific world-view: the dualism of referring expression and referent... of sentence and fact, theory and data, language and world, culture and nature. The presentation of literature as the quasi-negation of this ontology changes nothing. The dualism of reference still functions as its conceptual starting point, its *arche*.[43]

Miller's claim is sufficiently sweeping to make the modest philosopher cringe, but there is a truth in it. The humanist's sceptic trades in this dualism Miller identifies: it is the distinction with which he inserts the wedge between world-constructing and world-imaging texts, between uses of words that latch onto the world and those that do not. And with little effort we can see how this underlies both drifts' expression of the sceptic's insight that what is outside the literary text is beyond the reach of the words of the text. Both drifts accept, implicitly or otherwise, that, for language to be informative of—to be *about*— the extra-linguistic, it must build a bridge between word and world (via reference, correspondence, representation, uniting signifier with signified, and so on). It is irrelevant that the poststructuralist makes the global claim that this bridge can *never* be built, be it in literary language or standard everyday speech. The arguments of the humanist's sceptic get afoot before any answer we might give to this question of whether language can (really, and so on) reveal reality. They flow directly from the question itself. This division of word and world into distinct realms that require bridging if language is to touch reality—regardless of whether or not one believes the bridge can actually be built—is the source of the sceptic's view of literature: *this* is what gives him the picture of the world and word relation upon which he begins his recital.

The humanist claims that poststructuralists just look like philosophers of the analytic drift who happen to have a much more despairing stance towards global epistemological and linguistic questions. While this may be of severe importance in other areas of

---

[43] Eric Miller (1996: 475).

philosophical concern—it has rather nasty consequences in epistemology and metaphysics, to name but a few—it means very little to the philosopher of literature interested in defending humanism. At the end of the day, philosophers of literature of the analytic and poststructuralist drifts look to the humanists to bed with one another: in both cases we begin with the word–world picture the sceptic exploits and end with the sceptic's view that literary texts bring fictions and fictions alone to view. The problem of literary language unites natural foes, or at any rate two drifts we often take to express radically uncomplimentary philosophical visions. In short, the two major movements in contemporary literary aesthetics give us virtually no tools for defending humanism; indeed they have developed vocabularies for speaking about literature that have made it virtually impossible to see how we might effectively speak like humanists.

The arguments against the possibility of direct-humanism we have been examining in this chapter are often described as arguments for the 'self-referentiality' of literary texts, and I want to point out a confusion in this way of putting the matter before going on. We can accept that literary language does not refer to anything external to the text, that in some sense it speaks about its own creations. But this does not imply that the words and descriptions of a text are in any literal sense self-referential. The concept of self-reference, though it has a perfectly normal everyday use (to capture the idea that a work of literary fiction describes its own world and not ours, for example), defies philosophical use here. Honest cases of self-reference require something like token-reflexivity ('this is a lie', said in reference not to another statement but to itself), and all literary language cannot, obviously, be assimilated to a case of token-reflexivity.[44]

What is meant by claiming that the language of literary fiction is self-referential can be captured with more philosophical insight by claiming that literature turns out to look very much like *a localized*

---

[44] I am here following Eric Miller's arguments against the self-referentiality of literature. See Eric Miller (1996).

case of the way in which the idealist views the world. The sceptic's position gives us a picture of literature as semantically isolated in the way in which the linguistic idealist's words are 'isolated': the world of the text is a mere construct of the words of the text (as the linguistic idealist believes the 'objects' of reference to be linguistic constructs). In normal uses of language, uses that bring us into contact with the world, some actual feature of the real world is the target of our words—its terminus, as it were. In literary texts we find only more and more words when we ask about the objects of reference: we can never break out of the text and ground the semantic reach of those words in something our-worldly.

Unless we find an alternative to common ways of speaking about the fictions we find in literature, and the nature of literary language more generally, we will have great trouble avoiding a position I trust no one except the most recalcitrant formalist or practitioner of literary aestheticism would willingly embrace—what I will call *literary isolationism*. Literary isolationism is not so much one theory among many we might endorse as a position we assume, by default as it were, when we find ourselves unable to say something sensible about how we can make sense of the humanist intuition. For, if we cannot explain how a work of fiction can bring reality to view, we will be extremely hard pressed to state exactly *where* in a novel we can find this layer of the our-worldly the humanist wants to read for. We will, that is, have invited a picture of literature, not as without *any* connection to reality (a claim that would probably be incoherent as well as mad), but as at least without a point of contact significant enough to make the project of developing the humanist intuition appear worthwhile.

In this respect the humanist's sceptic shows himself to be a literary isolationist. Of course, the sceptic allows for certain points of contact between literary texts and reality. But, as we have seen, they are either of trivial benefit to the humanist (sameness of *Sinn*) or have no proper literary significance (indirect humanism; the use of reality in constructing literary setting and scenario). The sceptic isolates the text from any *significant* connection, from any direct point of contact that is interesting from both the perspective of the world and that of the literary work. He puts forth the constraint that we must speak of what we find in a literary work when describing the significance of a literary text, that we must base what we say about it on what we find *in* it. In short, he shows us that we must respect its autonomy (as is easily done by making the world of a literary text a *sui generis* possible or imagined world, or by claiming that 'il n'y a pas de'hors-texte'). And he points out that, once we speak from the standpoint of the literary, we find that, with every attempt to touch external reality, we trip over literature's fictionality or run up against its textual autonomy. Unless he finds another route, the humanist is defeated by the sceptic's isolationism, left with the sceptic's idealist picture of literary language. And all this is done on the force of the sceptic's simple and reasonable claim that none of the requisite semantic acts guides the language we find in the literary work of art.

2

Literature and the Sense of the World

Of all the uses of language we have developed, the literary has some claim to being the most liberated. It speaks in freedom from the truth and the facts, and it is largely unconstrained by the very world that our other, less elevated uses of language struggle to represent. It is a remarkable feature of human linguistic development that we have devised a use of language that can be intensely meaningful and engaging yet say nothing about the very thing we presumably developed language to navigate better: the world.

The sceptic brings to our attention that this liberty the literary enjoys from the real implies that there is something quite peculiar about the humanist intuition. If the humanist wants to say that literature makes claims about reality, the sceptic argues that there is no semantic device we can invoke to explain how this might be possible. So the humanist seems to be silenced, left without a word to say about how a work of literary fiction can speak about reality. Unless we are willing to summon the desperate category of the ineffable, as older versions of humanism were often content to do, and try to make a convenient virtue out of this silence, we have to give the sceptic his due.[1] He is both convincing and reasonable, and this much should be granted him.

---

[1] The allusion here is to the Scrutinists' notion of 'Life' and the New Critics' notion of the 'Concrete Universal' and 'The Eternal', both of which have taints of the ineffable. The idea in both cases is that the vision (of 'life'; of the 'eternal') offered by the text are inseparable from the text itself. This in turn implies that there is no explaining these insights by way of paraphrasing the text into an argument or interpreting it until we can elicit a (detachable, as it were) proposition. We can just present someone with the text and say that either she gets it or she doesn't (somewhat as we say that we cannot *show*

So the humanist appears—at this point at least—to be without any linguistic resource for describing how a use of language can have a worldly object when it fails to run along those semantic rails that connect language and reality. We do not have worldly reference, truth, representation (and soon), and thus we have no clear way of explaining how literary texts might reveal reality in their descriptions of their own imaginatively created characters and events. We can, along with the indirect humanist, console ourselves by remarking on literature's ability to hint at and in various ways suggest stances towards the real. But we also saw that this is of no substantial literary significance, that it takes us away from the literary work rather than brings us closer to it. What we saw that the humanist needs, and what the sceptic appears to have shown he cannot have, is an *immediate* point of contact, a way of explaining how reality might be yielded directly in the literary use of language.

I think that we would do best to acquiesce and accept that the areas the sceptic's argument touched on are lost to the humanist. In fact, I would say that the sceptic has given a sense of the boundaries of any discussion of literary language, an idea of where we cannot go if we want to stay in touch with the literary. And I think that he is unequivocally correct to demand that we respect the autonomy of literature, that literary works are of value because of what we find when we explore their interior and not because of some external value they might lead us towards. Arguing for humanism in such a way that we turn literature into a mere springboard for connecting us to extra-literary reality would be a violence to the idea of the literary, to the practice of treating literary works as objects of appreciation in their own right.[2] So the question becomes: what is the humanist to do?

---

why a joke is funny apart from repeating the joke itself: no satisfactory discursive account of what makes it humorous is possible).

[2] The literary scholar Derek Attridge felicitously calls this view of the value of literature 'literary instrumentalism': 'What I have in mind could be crudely summarized as the treating of a text (or other cultural artifact) as a means to a predetermined end: coming to the object with the hope or assumption that it can be instrumental in

What one ought to do here is accept that we cannot show literature to be our-worldly in the respect the sceptic has denied it can be. It does not 'mirror' reality, it states no truths about it, its sentences do not correspond with it, and it is part of the very idea of literature that this be so. Instead, we try to support humanism along the lines of another picture altogether, giving up the tools the sceptic has argued are lost to the humanist. The humanist can let the sceptic's various arguments stand as they are: besides being persuasive, they are sincere expressions of the literary. The thorn is the picture of literature the sceptic believes follows from his recital, this picture of literary texts as in effect sketches of the idealist's vision of the world. In short, the trouble lies in his literary *isolationism*, the moral he draws from his recital. This is what I want to show that we can avoid, the isolationist picture of literature the sceptic draws from his various arguments.

It will take the remainder of this book to offer an adequate response to the sceptic. In this chapter I begin by examining the linguistic and semantic issues the sceptic raises in his recital. This will provide a foundation for approaching in the following chapters the epistemological, interpretative, and metaphysical issues that are also at play here.

2.1. THE PICTURE OF PARADOX

The sceptic's arguments make it look as though humanism is best described as built upon paradox, a desire to understand literature in terms of precisely what literature turns out to be contrasted with: a vision of the way the world is. Whatever else a paradox may be, when we are on the receiving end of one it means that we cannot say what we want because asserting so much appears to be senseless: our desideratum is unfortunately also an impossibility. So far the sceptic has told us this: the humanist intuition is paralysed because

---

furthering an existing project, and responding to it in such a way as to test, or even produce that usefulness' (Attridge 2004: 7).

language offers no way to develop this intuition: a use of language that has neither worldly truth nor reference cannot make claims about reality, indeed in no significant sense can be about it. So embracing humanism appears to demand—and here lies the sense of paradox—that we cast literature as engaged in an exploration of the very thing it turns its back on: reality.

Yet exactly why should we feel the presence of paradox here? Why should the humanist appear to be faced with an impossibility? The sceptic responds by simply repeating his recital: he tells us that he has already answered this question. But with a moment's reflection we can see that isolationism does not fall in fine logical fashion from the sceptic's recital, as, say, idealism does from Berkeley's *esse est percipi*. In the latter case, the position is implied by the very words used to state the argument: it just says so much. The same is not true of the sceptic's isolationism. Saying that literature has neither worldly truth nor reference does not in any straightforward sense just amount to the claim that there is *no* significant point of contact between world and literary work. All the humanist asks for is a *substantial* point of contact, and nowhere in the characterization of his intuition were the words 'truth' or 'reference' used, no precise commitments to the mode of contact between work and world were made. Thus there is an implicit assumption we need to unearth. We need to ask what gives us this sense that isolationism is a consequence of the sceptic's recital.

As with most cases in which we feel the presence of paradox without quite seeing its source, there is a larger picture in place, exerting its force on us from behind the scenes. This is what I think is happening here. There is another commitment, some more basic picture, by virtue of which the sceptic's arguments strike us as leading so easily to literary isolationism. We know that what summons the picture of literary isolationism are the sceptic's arguments against the presence of worldly truth and reference in literature. Yet what makes us think that we have no significant worldly contact without them? What makes us think that the humanist is silenced just because of their absence?

Whatever the exact picture the sceptic embraces may be, at least this much is clear: in it we find a general commitment to the essential role of *representation* in explaining how a use of language, a description, an image, can be *about* the world. This is a quite natural commitment, given how much philosophy of language endorses it in one form or another. But it is also very dangerous, especially if taken to mark the exclusive means of building a bridge between a sentence or an image and reality. In the philosophy of language, this can easily lead to the mistaken belief that there are two basic uses of language, that in which language represents some actual state of affairs and is therefore informative of how things stand in the world, and that in which it does not, in which case it is, if not just so much nonsense, at least not revelatory of anything that could go by the name of reality (something many verificationist and positivistic strands of twentieth-century philosophy were content to claim). In literary aesthetics, this commitment to representation surfaces in a strikingly similar sense that we have two and only two alternatives. Consider the following passage from J. Hillis Miller's recent *On Literature*: 'A literary work is not, as many people may assume, an imitation in words of some pre-existing reality but, on the contrary, it is the creation of a new, supplementary world, a metaworld, a hyper-reality.'[3] What Miller describes as the assumption that literature is an 'imitation of pre-existing reality' is what the history of aesthetics calls the *mimetic* theory of art—namely, the theory that casts art as a representation of extra-literary reality, the so-called mirror view of art. And notice what the alternatives are, at least as Miller frames them: either literature is mimetic, in which case it shows us our world; or it brings to view a newly created world, a *hyper*-reality, which, whatever else it might be, presumably is not quite *our* reality. How odd that there should not be anything other than these two options.

---

[3] J. Hillis Miller (2002: 18).

Since the 1960s there has hardly been anyone willing to endorse a genuinely mimetic theory of literary fiction,[4] to claim that fictions in any proper sense of the term *represent* reality.[5] Indeed, the sceptic's recital can be read as just an abridged version of common ways of dismissing mimetic and representational theories of literature. But the problem—the heart of the problem, I think—is that we tend to hear the rejection of the representational theory of art as an implicit denial of the idea that literature can bear an internal link to the real. This is what claims such as Miller's play upon. For, in giving up the representational picture of literature, we abandon the very thing so many aestheticians and literary theorists tell us we need if we are to give support to the idea that art can be revelatory of reality.

What the sceptic exploits in his recital is the common idea that the semantic tools he has taken from the humanist are the only tools with which one can construct a bridge between language and extra-linguistic reality. But to accept this is to betray that one is in the grip of a certain picture of how word and world are basically hooked up. It is, in effect, the old idea of a *divide in kind* between language (or thought) and reality, a divide that requires the semantic tools the sceptic has taken from the humanist to be crossed. It is that pervasive but unsettling idea of a 'gap' that informs many of philosophy of language's basic dualisms, between (to play on the famous Sellarsian distinction[6]) the logical space of nature and the logical space of language, between the things we talk about and the things in themselves, between the natural and the conventional, between word and world. The sceptic's argument that these semantic

---

[4] To be more precise, the terms 'mimesis' and 'representation' are still used in contemporary aesthetics, especially of the analytical variety. But these terms have come to designate the ways in which literary works represent *fictional* worlds. Thus 'mimesis' and 'representation' have in their contemporary usage been severed from the traditional humanist use of these terms to explain how literary works represent reality.

[5] For an interesting and well-argued exception, see Nuttall (1983).

[6] It is actually McDowell who puts the Sellars in this Sellarsian distinction. McDowell (1996) describes his distinction between the logical space of nature and the logical space of reasons as Sellarsian in spirit, which it certainly is. What Sellars actually spoke about was the logical space of reason, without the complementary 'nature' side of McDowell's distinction.

tools are unavailable to the humanist has so much force because of the role these tools play in this picture. They are *the* tools for bringing language to bear on reality, and so one naturally feels that the humanist is lost when they are taken from him. On this picture, literature looks to be just that use of language that most plainly reveals this gap between language and reality; it seems to be a testament to its existence.[7] For what better proof might we have of the ability of language to be parsed apart from reality than the literary use of language? If a picture of this sort is in place, it just seems natural to think that in those cases where language fails or refuses to represent reality—say the language of literary fiction—we appear to be left with *mere* language, words without any worldly point of contact.[8]

The idea of a divide between language and reality is at best metaphorical, though two thousand years of debates between idealists and realists have provided many occasions to invoke the picture of a separation in kind between the linguistic and the real. I would think that this picture can be illustrated in a great number of ways, but for our purposes we might express it as follows. It tells us that language and world are separated by a window, if you like. When language speaks about reality, it looks out of the window and describes what it sees. It attempts to mirror or, as it is more commonly put, represent what is on the other side of the window. When we explain the relationship between a linguistic representation and its object, we

---

[7] This much was suggested in Sections 1.1 and 1.2 when I examined the sceptic's argument that without reference we have mere sense, words with meaning but no worldly involvement.

[8] This picture not only lies implicit in claims like J. Hillis Miller's, claims that are representative of how a considerable swath of theory and philosophy of literature speaks about the nature of imaginative literature. It has also been an explicit feature of theorizing about literature in certain strands of literary theory since the 1940s. We see find it in the tradition of francophone theory leading from Georges Bataille and Maurice Blanchot to Jacques Derrida and Paul de Man. Literature here is cast as just that textual form which reveals this divide between word and world and thus testifies to the distance between them (rather than attempts to overcome it). It is this tradition that gave rise to the still fashionable claim (in some circles at least) that literature is more honest than philosophy, for at least it is forthcoming about its fictionality. See Weston (2001) for a very helpful discussion of this tradition.

invoke the common distinctions between a referring expression and its referent, a word and the bit of the world to which it corresponds; reality and our sentential renderings of it. We look through the window and use our words to mirror, like verbal landscape sketchers, what we see. On this picture the idea of wedding word and world becomes a question of representational accomplishment, of whether what we say when we look out of the window is a fair portrait of how things stand on the other side of it.[9]

We can see, as I hinted in the discussion of the analytic and poststructuralist drifts, why traditional realist and idealist standpoints—standpoints that in various ways endorse this idea of a divide—are so inimical to the humanist. It is commonplace to speak of traditional linguistic idealism and realism as revolving around the same axis, around what is best described as a representationalist view of our connection to the world. The realist, to put it crudely, emphasizes the plausibility of the idea that our semantic tools actually enable speakers to build bridges between their words and their world: he has faith in both the view we have from the window and in language's ability to describe what is on the other side of it. He trusts in reference to yield worldly referents, representations to unite us with the worldly objects they picture. The idealist (at least of the sceptical and anti-realist variety), again to put it crudely, argues that as far as we have the right to claim the window might just as well

---

[9] I use these metaphors of maps, mirrors, and windows as a way of explaining traditional realism and idealism as it is found in various 'representational', 'metaphysical', or 'transcendental' interpretations of these positions. Crispin Wright gives an excellent characterization of the picture that underlies these views. 'A reasonable pre-theoretical characterization of realism about, say, the external world seems to me that it . . . concerns the *independence* of the external world—for example, that the external world exists independently of us, that it is independent of the conceptual vocabulary in terms of which we think about it, and that it is independent of the beliefs about it which we do, will, could, ever form. Fully fledged, modesty has it that human thought is, at best, a *map* of the world' (Wright 1992: 1–2). We are speaking about language rather than thought, but the idea is the same. On this score, idealism as I describe it here (as the sceptical, anti-realist strain of idealism) would be a position that accepts this picture and merely takes a sceptical stance towards our ability to justify any talk that presupposes the adequacy of the 'map'. I refer, when needed, to these traditional positions as expressed as a point about the word–world relation as *linguistic realism* and *linguistic idealism*.

be a mirror; he argues that all we are justified in claiming is that our representations are reflections of our own linguistic categories and conventions, yielding a view of what is on our side of the window rather than the objects the realist believes are on the other side of it.

Both standpoints make humanism an impossible position.[10] In the idealist's world we don't have the right to speak of literature as connecting us to the world because *no* use of language does: idealism makes all uses of language resemble the sceptic's isolationist view of literature and so it is of no help to the humanist's search to find reality in literature. Certainly, in the idealist's world literature would still be contrasted with uses of language that function to refer to and represent the 'facts' of our linguistically constructed reality,[11] and thus the sceptic can simply repeat his recital in the vocabulary of an idealist (something philosophers such as Richard Rorty, who think that embracing anti-realism will help vindicate literature, fail to see[12]). On the traditional realist picture, humanism is also made senseless. For reasons we are already aware of, literary language just shows itself to fail to function in step with those uses of language that have access to the window. In short, it is irrelevant whether we take a realist or an idealist stance towards the supposed divide that runs between word and world, for, as long as we countenance this picture of a divide that can be crossed only by way of representation, humanism is a hopeless position.

---

[10] See Simon Critchley (2005) for an interesting discussion of how the 'philosophical' poetry of the mature Wallace Stevens maps out an alternative to linguistic realism and anti-realism: 'So, in my view Stevens is philosophically significant because his verse recasts the basic problem of epistemology in a way that perhaps allows to the problem to be cast away. What we might call his "poetic epistemology" can be said to place in question the assumptions behind the traditional epistemological construal of the world' (Critchley 2005: 30).

[11] I discuss this in detail in Chapter 5 when I examine the thesis of 'panfictionalism'. By 'facts of our constructed linguistic reality' I am drawing attention to the fact that even the most recalcitrant constructivist would admit that we do not confuse the story of a novel with actual history (however the anti-realist conceives of 'history'), and thus there is still a contrast between fictional and non-fictional uses of language in the idealist's universe.

[12] See Boghossian (2006) for a compelling criticism of Rortian versions of constructivist anti-realism.

As entrenched as this representationalist picture of the word–world relation may be, it is not compulsory. In fact, though it is not quite wrong, it is an astonishingly *incomplete* picture. What needs to be pointed out here is something simple, perhaps obvious, but that has an unfortunate tendency to be overlooked in these debates. What I have in mind is this: even if it is the case that representation and reference account for one of the ways in which we bring language to bear on reality, it certainly is not the only way. Stronger still, it cannot even be the basic way. There are other forms of linguistic involvement with reality, forms that must already be in place for representation and reference to be possible. In other words, the important question that is left unasked on this picture is: *what sort of prior connections between language and reality must be in place to account for the very fact that language can represent and refer to reality?* If we frame the issue in this way, we begin by asking how it might be possible to see our language as in some (as yet unspecified) sense hooking up to reality before representation, that the union, if it can be called that, takes places elsewhere, at any rate long before we use sentences to represent reality. To approach the issue this way is not to deny that language can 'map' reality but to push back questions of reference, representation, and correspondence to only certain types of world-informed uses of language. In so doing, it brings into view possibilities of linguistic involvement with reality ignored on the sceptic's representationalist model of the word–world relation, possibilities I shall argue literature is especially well suited to explore. What I ultimately hope to show is that this will allow us to overcome the picture that is presupposed in the reasoning that makes literary language look like an oddity and humanism an impossibility.

To help my argument along I will make use of the philosophy of the later Wittgenstein. Few philosophers divide a room as quickly as Wittgenstein. I am not entirely sure why this is, but I shall use Wittgenstein in such a way as to retain what many philosophers find attractive in his philosophy and leave aside what many find dated or contentious. I have no interest in the bogeyman of behaviourism, the elusiveness of the psychological 'inner', or whether Robinson

Crusoe might possess a private language. What I think remains of considerable value in Wittgenstein's philosophy is his attempt to remove much of the metaphysical scaffolding from our understanding of the workings of language and his efforts to replace it with a thoroughly *social, cultural* conception of language. It is this social story of how we put language in contact with reality that I am interested in here and that I think will help us see something important about literature. It is a story that could just as easily be told in the vocabulary of many diverse movements in contemporary philosophy of language. I choose Wittgenstein's version of this story because of its familiarity as well as on account of the role it has played in bringing about this shift from the metaphysical to the social in contemporary Anglo-American philosophy of language.

2.2. THE PARIS ARCHIVE

It might be wise to begin by situating this discussion in a more basic matter of philosophical interest, what we might refer to, initially at least, as *the wonder of agreement*. We share, to a rather astonishing degree, similar patterns of linguistic response and description. We by and large call the same things by the same names, and we perceive the world in the same general hues: *this* expanse of sky is blue, *that* patch of earth is lush, *this* gesture counts as an expression of delight, *that* shrug announces indifference. This does not mean that we always say the same things about the world. We differ as a matter of daily course in how we describe various regions of our world. But the very possibility of disagreement points up the existence of a broad backdrop of agreement, a shared stage upon which we can rehearse our differences. If it were not for this broad backdrop of agreement, our encounters with contrarians, nay-sayers, and other disputatious sorts would result in unintelligibility rather than debate, and for better or worse this is rarely the case. In this respect, disagreements in how we talk about the world have the unexpected effect of revealing as much commonality as disunity. What, then, is it that we possess in common that accounts for this general agreement with one another in speech? In what does this basic alignment consist?

One of the ways of expressing the attraction Wittgenstein holds for philosophers of an anti-metaphysical bent is that he offers what is arguably the first thoroughly cultural response to this question. Wittgenstein thought that much philosophy goes astray—becomes a form of 'nonsense', as he liked to put it—in response to the question of how this general alignment is possible. If a proper account of the wonder of agreement requires that we explain precisely *what* is shared among us, the standpoint philosophy has baptized 'Platonism' might be seen as attempting to explain this in terms of metaphysical entities, say a common grasp of an Idea or of an item in the Realm of Sense. Not only Platonism, but what we often take to be its contrary, empiricism, is often guilty of a similar offence, positing something 'given' in experience—for example, 'sense-data' that produce common concepts in each of us. Wittgenstein's philosophical method was one of trying to exorcize from philosophy its traditional reliance on metaphysical theses, and this required, he thought, that we erase from philosophical explanations all reference to occult entities, 'queer' objects, and the like.

The closest thing Wittgenstein offers philosophy as a method for finding a way away from the metaphysical and back to the rough ground of the cultural is his notion of a 'perspicuous representation':[13]

A main source of our failure to understand is that we do not *command a clear view* of the use of our words.—Our grammar is lacking in this sort of perspicuity. A perspicuous representation produces just that understanding which consists in 'seeing connections'. Hence the importance of finding and inventing *intermediate cases*. The concept of a perspicuous representation is

---

[13] Or a perspicuous 'presentation': the German is *darstellung*. Although Wittgenstein scholars now appear to prefer to translate it with 'presentation' rather than 'representation', I will remain with the standard translation here.

of fundamental importance for us. It earmarks the forms of the account we give, the way we look at things.[14]

A 'failure to understand' in philosophy is remedied by presenting an example of a way of engaging in the activity in question (for example, a way of applying a concept, of following a rule, of grasping a new sense) but in such a way that nothing seems strange, nothing appears to stand in need of explanation. In fact a perspicuous representation does not quite *explain* anything. It rather demystifies what we once found 'queer'—a perspicuous representation takes, if you like, the wonder out of our wonderings. It does not do so by revealing what goes on in *every* instance of the activity we want to understand clearly, as though a perspicuous representation offers a God's-eye view of our practices, an insight into something like their common essence. They do not have one. Perspicuous representations rather act as 'intermediate cases' in the sense that in them we see presented a picture of human activity that appears to be of a piece with the practice that once seemed problematic, only now without the attendant sense of wonder, only now without the sense that something stands in need of explanation. We thus see suggested in a perspicuous representation a possibility for how we might regard our *actual* practices in a similar light, for how to turn back to them and see them clearly.

To return to the question of agreement, consider the 'Paris archive' passage in the *Philosophical Investigations*, which I take to offer a model case of what Wittgenstein means by a perspicuous representation.

There is *one* thing of which one can say neither that it is one metre long, nor that it is not one metre long, and that is the standard metre in Paris. —But this is, of course, not to ascribe any extraordinary property to it, but only to mark its peculiar role in the language-game of measuring with a metre-rule. —Let us imagine samples of colour being preserved in Paris like the standard metre. We define: 'sepia' means

---

[14] Wittgenstein (2001: §122).

the colour of the standard sepia which is there kept hermetically sealed. Then it will make no sense to say of this sample either that it is of this colour or that it is not. We can put it like this: This sample is an instrument of the language used in ascriptions of colour. In this language-game it is not something that is represented, but is an instrument of representation... It is a standard in our language-game, something with which a comparison is made. And this may be an important observation, but it is nonetheless an observation concerning our language game—our method of representation.[15]

What is of interest in this passage for our purposes is that it presents a thoroughly demystified picture of how we come to possess commonly what is required for the existence of a representational practice: for having shared ways of rendering the world in thought and speech. If the fact of agreement appeared incredible, a thing of wonder, the above example presents it as something altogether mundane. We are able to represent items in our world as counting as a metre long not because all those who engage in this practice have access to a common metaphysical item. It is because of a prior cultural act, an initial moment of social production, that this is possible: the creation of public *standards* of representation, the construction of common cultural instruments with which we can then go on to engage in the building of representations of our world.

What is crucial in the above passage is that the standard metre is archived. It is the idea of an archive that is supposed to bring to clarity what some philosophers have thought only a metaphysical thesis could explain. This is because the idea of an archive shows us how to tell the story of agreement without invoking anything 'queer,' anything extra-cultural. It functions to draw our attention to the *institutional* setting of language and the possibility that agreement is grounded upon something fully public. When Wittgenstein goes on to imagine a 'standard sepia' in the Paris archive, we are not asked to see our practice of representing the world in colours as resting upon samples preserved in any one archive, needless to say. Wittgenstein

[15] Ibid. §50.

here draws attention to the fact that he is describing an 'intermediate case', and we are expected to turn from it and see that explaining our representational practices generally can be carried out in a similar fashion. That is, we are expected to go on and consider *our* archives, or those features of our public world that amount to them. We are expected to look for the *actual* places in which we store our instruments of representation. We are not asked to consider some oddity such as a 'colour archive' but to recall, for example, that a standard colour chart can be found with ease in art supplies and hardware stores.

Note that, when Wittgenstein describes the standard metre as neither a metre long nor *not* a metre long,[16] he is not ascribing 'any extraordinary property to it', because he is not speaking of a property at all. He is rather describing the *role* the standard metre has in the practice of measurement. There is nothing more to say about whether a certain length counts as a metre if we hold it up to standard metre in the Paris archive. And there is nothing more to say precisely because the standard metre is not a representation of some further thing that accounts for its being a metre long: it is the *very* thing that explains what it means to be a metre long. We cannot call it a 'real instance' of a metre, because it is not *an instance* of anything (of Metre-ness, or whatever it might be). But, for all that, it is not *unreal*, a *fiction* of a metre. It is crucially real, and its existence explains the possibility of an entire (as Hayden White might say) 'tropic of discourse'—namely, talk of measuring the world in terms of metres. To make explicit the general point this announces, when we examine our standards of representation, we are inspecting things that are obviously real though not representations of anything real at all.

---

[16] This is a claim Kripke (1980) found especially puzzling, and his critique of it is still well regarded by many in the philosophical community. Since none of I what wish to take from Wittgenstein rides on whether we should want, with Kripke, to say that the Paris metre-rule in the end really is a metre long, I ignore this area of debate. What I take from this example is the idea of a *standard* of representation, and I have no further interest in questions of rigid designation and the like.

In this sense, the connection between language and reality is much deeper than we notice if we approach the issue only by way of wondering how words might map or mirror the world. Of course we do represent the world in speech, refer to it, say things that 'correspond' to it. What Wittgenstein wants is not to deny the possibility of extra-linguistic representation. His interest here is to prod us to explore the links to reality presupposed by the fact that sentences can represent and refer to it. This is in effect what his example of the Paris metre answers, though in characteristically anecdotal form. That is, the example functions to bring to light the moment of cultural activity that makes possible patterns of mutual alignment in speech, of how we can enjoy access in thought and speech to a common world. This, I take it, is the upshot of the example of the Paris archive: to understand the basic association between word and world one must offer an account of how a culture builds its linguistic practices upon something public, and so something it then can go on to use as shared instruments—shared standards—for speaking about the world.

In this respect it might be more accurate to say that we apply *world to world by way of language* in representation than that we merely apply word to world; and we should hear this claim as running contrary to the notion that representation explains the basic, initial if you like, union of language and reality. We account for this not by claiming that language can perform some mysterious metaphysical act. We rather show that the story of the source of our standards for talking about the world is a tale of cultural activity, a matter of how we develop standards of representation by building words upon our world: upon our encounters with, and attempts to give voice to, the objects we encounter, the range of human activity we witness, and the spectrum of experiences we suffer.

The full story of how language comes to use the world as a standard of representation will be quite complex. In the case of simple objects such as chairs and rocks, the story may be the fairly familiar one of coming to name an object and agreeing on the name we have given it—more complicated, but perhaps not too interestingly so, than what we find in the example of the Paris archive. In the case of our more complex terms such as 'personhood', 'goodness', 'love', and so on, the story will probably boil down to social history. Jealousy, to give an (overly) simple example, develops conceptually and linguistically as our culture develops institutionally. We develop institutions based on the pledge of fidelity (such as marriage); and, once we have public and so transmittable examples of people betraying these institutions, we can use the behaviour of the wounded (Dido of Virgil's *Aeneas*, for example) as a standard by which we can, so to speak, go on to represent the world jealously.

These patterns of agreement are expressive of what are sometimes called linguistic *criteria*, a term I will make great use of when I return to literature. This is what the construction and sharing of standards of representation make possible: our ability to have a criterial, and so normative, way of rendering our world. Our descriptions of reality are made possible in part by the fact that we possess these shared criteria. They explain how it is that we are able to speak in a common tongue of anything as being *this* sort of thing: how it is that we are able to 'word the world together'.[17] Criteria do not 'make it the case' that the world is really as we say it is or 'establish the truth' of what language calls reality. They provide the conditions of mutual intelligibility and so of any sort of talk at all, truth talk included. Indeed, the notions of criteria and standards of representation enjoy a sort of priority over the notions of truth and representation, for it is only in virtue of them that we have standards for adjudicating our truth claims, our claims to knowledge: they offer us those standards by which our claims to have represented the world correctly in assertive speech ('this is a metre') can be open to scrutiny. The significance of these claims will become clearer as we proceed, but the immediate point is that criteria function not as a sort of replacement to talk of representation and correspondence. They designate the bedrock of meaningful talk, of what must be in place socially for a general alignment in language to be possible.

[17] Cavell (1979: 316).

If a social account of language along these lines is compelling, we can see that, when we give an account of our common language (rather than of the things we use language to talk about), we are not recording facts about an impersonal structure of symbols and sounds that we just happen to find ourselves with. It is not, in other words, to give an account of something that is pure *Sinn*, language with no involvement with extra-linguistic 'life'. To give an account of our language is in an important respect to give account of ourselves, of the way in which a sign is given life by what Wittgenstein calls our 'form of life', a phrase that brings home the idea that language is not a mere grammatical system but is itself an expression of the our-worldly. In this respect, one of the clearest insights we can aspire to have into the way our world is is achieved by bringing to view the standards of representation, the criteria, our culture has developed in its efforts to forge a shared sense of its world. It is by reflecting on them that we can read the story of what a culture has come to call its world.

This grounding of language upon shared criteria and standards of representation (as I will use them, there is no important difference between these terms) does not imply that there is a monolithic standard of meaningful speech, and it is important to see this, lest we hear all this as suggesting the absurd idea that we all must always say the same things about the world when we apply our language to it (as though an argument or debate always implies that one of the parties does not understand language or has not been fully initiated into our 'form of life'). We differ in all sorts of obvious ways in how we describe various corners of our world, we find ourselves with at times incompatible standards of representation, and we are in a constant processing of refining, abandoning and inventing criteria. The idea here is not that we all must possess the same criteria (though we must have many in common if local disagreement in criteria can be intelligibly expressed). What we should be unwilling to do is to let variations in what we say lead to a crude form of relativism that threatens to undermine the idea of a basic shared alignment with reality. We do encounter people who speak about the world in ways we would not, such as when I meet an animist or an AI theorist. But I do not thereby parse people apart into those who share my world and those who seem to be aligned with another one altogether just on account of these variances. I may doubt someone who offers a refashioning of the flat-earth theory; I do not doubt that we stand on the same earth when we debate this. My attitude towards these points of disagreement and variations in belief and speech is much like the one I have when I speak to a child or a genius: I see a deficit or depth of perception *in confronting the same world*. If an analogy is needed, our attitude towards the alignment given expression in our criteria and standards of representations is like that we have towards the ground we walk on rather than a hypothesis we may debate.[18] It is presupposed in the act of speaking meaningfully to one another rather than an abstract theoretical hypothesis. The attempt to undermine the idea of commonality in meaning and reality in the way certain arguments for crude versions of relativism do—generalizing from local disagreements and errors to the possibility that from beginning to end we might be aligned with different 'worlds' or 'realities'—fails to take into consideration that the very pointing-up of errors and differences in vocabularies and commitments already betrays a basic common alignment, an alignment that is revealed by the brute fact that we succeed in making our differences understood to one another.[19]

---

[18] I borrow here from Lars Hertzberg's phrase 'faith in the ground we walk on'. See Hertzberg (1976: 150).

[19] Much more can be said against the idea that local errors (say when we find that a scientific or moral picture is wrong) can be generalized into the 'mightn't we be wrong about everything else' hypothesis we find in garden-variety sceptical arguments. This debate is much too involved for my purposes here, and so I leave it aside. But a suggestion for an argument that would be consistent with what I have said above might be the following: we cannot generalize from a failure of a local vocabulary (say of a failed but once entrenched scientific theory) to a claim about the possibility of error in all other areas. In attempting this, the sceptic fails to see, as Michael Williams puts it, 'the context-sensitivity of both sceptical doubts and everyday certainties' by mistakenly assuming that one can investigate (or generalize about) 'our epistemic situation', as though it is a sort of unified field of inquiry (Michael Williams 1991: 35).

2.3. NARRATING THE WORLD

To return to literature, it is first worth pointing out that we can now see that a textual form such as literary fiction that offers no representations of reality will not on that count alone be isolated from reality. There are, that is, other possibilities of worldly involvement. What I have done is to replace the picture the sceptic exploits with one in which language is seen not as connecting to an independent reality exclusively by representing it but at a more direct level, in its standards of representation, its criteria. What I hope now appears plausible is that this allows us to see the connection between language and reality as prior (in understanding, as Aristotle might say) to the level at which the sceptic gives his arguments. If so, there should no longer be the sense that isolationism necessarily follows from the sceptic's recital, no more force behind the sceptic's argument that we are left with *mere* language if we lose worldly reference and representation. The wedding of word and world does not take place exclusively at the level the sceptic envisioned; thus nothing is necessarily divided when we lose the semantic tools and devices he argued are unavailable to the humanist. And, if this is so, the humanist is not obviously beset with paradox when he claims that literature, presenting to view words unconcerned with the stirrings of extra-textual reality, can present us with something sufficient to bring our world to light.

But this excursion into the philosophy of language gives us something more important. It also provides us with a vocabulary with which to start giving shape to the humanist intuition, a vocabulary that can help us begin to explain what sort of view of social and cultural reality literature can put on offer. I will conclude this chapter by shedding some light on this, offering a constellation of reflections that I shall shape into respectable insights in the following chapters. While what I say here will require further elaboration, I want to say something about the possibilities that have now opened up for the humanist.

What I will call the 'basic humanist claim', the ground-level statement we are now entitled to make about the presence of the real in literature, can be characterized as follows. We want to say that, for some aspect of a work of literature that arouses our worldly interest, we can claim of it that '*this* is ϕ' in such a way that there is no significant wedge to be placed between the fiction's presentation of ϕ and what ϕ is. We take the demonstrative as functioning to pick out not a represented worldly object (the sceptic has taken this from us) nor a creature of pure fiction (which the sceptic says it must pick out) but something more directly real, say, for the moment, ϕ just as it is. For those aspects of cultural life that fuel the furnaces of literary creation, we want to say that they are *seen*, just as they are, in the text: that *this* is jealousy, *this* is anger, *this* is suffering, and so on. And we want to be able to say this in such a way that the force of the demonstrative is one of identifying directly within the literary work something more properly called life than the merely lifelike, the world rather than a fictional mimesis of it.

How does the previous discussion help us say this? As a first pass at this, consider for a moment not our practice of measuring with metres or representing the world in colour but something more complex. Consider instead those words that are crucial to our more cultural renderings of our world. Think of those terms and concepts that describe significant sorts of human activity and response, that bring to view ways in which human lives can assume significance, come undone, thrive. Think of terms like 'love' or 'suffering', 'exploitation' or 'devotion', or of our ability to cast ourselves and others as in possession of this or that sort of self, of our ability to depict others in very precise shades of moral, political, and cultural identity.

How is it that we can represent reality in these hues, that we can describe features of our world as expressive of or otherwise falling under these concepts? Unlike the standard metre, these words—rather, these features of human circumstance (they are obviously much more than just words)—would seem to have no corresponding 'object' that could be archived. They designate extremely complex representational practices, at any rate sufficiently more complex than measuring with a metre-rule. And, if the story of agreement, of how we can come to represent the word commonly, requires the existence of public standards of representations, what could possibly act as our standards for terms and concepts such as these? They are grounded not on 'things' or 'objects' at all but upon very elaborate visions of human life. And how could something like *that* be archived? We can imagine a sample of sepia being placed next to the standard metre in the Paris archive. But what could we possibly imagine placing there to ground the practice of depicting certain items in the world as oppressed, as flourishing, as counting as an instance of joy?

The response I think one should give to these questions is that it is a culture's possession of a narrative tradition that documents the various stories we have to tell of ourselves that shows us how this could be. As soon as we recall what it means to have a literary heritage, we see that we have a culture full of 'objects' we can use to archive these stories. We have, that is, novels, plays, and poems. And we have places where we put them, public places: libraries, bookstores, classrooms, living rooms, and so on. The idea of a literary work is perhaps the clearest picture we have of how a culture can enjoy such refined, varied, and complex possibilities of perception and description. It is the institution of literature that brings to light most 'perspicuously', as Wittgenstein might say, how we can distil into a public object and thus make available to a culture generally something as intricate as a vision of life undone by, for example, jealousy and ambition. For we have *Othello*, and many more dramatic works in addition. Literature is not the only institution that plays a role in archiving these instruments of cultural representation—there are other art forms and other ways of telling stories. But the institution of literature brings to view the possibility of having such complex practices more clearly than any other institution in our culture.

Consider the complex vision of suffering one finds in Dostoevsky's *Notes from Underground,* where the sort of suffering he brings to our attention arises from a condition of mind in which one's self and one's world come to appear at once alien and revolting. It is a vision many critics claim is Dostoevsky's darker, Eastern European spin on what the British and German romantics identified as the problem of the 'modern world': its tendency to offer no meaningful possibilities of selfhood and human relationship and so to push us away from ourselves and others, into the 'Underground', which, whatever else the Underground might be, symbolizes something general and terrible about the human condition. Now Dostoevsky's creation represents no *actual* case of suffering, but, for all that, it is clearly not *nothing* we see when we read it, any more than a view of the standard metre in the Paris archive would be a glimpse of a purely imaginary metre. When we look at Dostoevsky's creation, we are regarding an object that is *constitutive* of a way in which we can see our world rather than mimetic duplication of it.

Of course, Notes from Underground does not mark the only way in which we can conceive suffering (many forms are hardly as complex as the Underground Man's). But, if we want to identify the various visions of suffering our culture makes available to us, the claim I am advancing is that we will do best to examine those texts that comprise our literary inheritance. We might begin, for example, with our tradition of tragic literature. At any rate, without Dostoevsky, and without our literary heritage more generally, we would not be able to see much of our world as we do, for literature is one of our practices that offers us the material out of which we can weave such intricate narratives of our way in the world. This is what it means to claim that something—some object, some image, some narrative—is a standard of representation. It is to claim that it opens up a way of seeing the world, and all that this implies.[20]

An image (in words, paint, or whatever) can 'stand for' reality without depicting it. One way in which this can happen—the way I am gesturing towards—is that it can perform a certain function—namely, that of being *representative* rather than

[20] David Schalkwyk and James Guetti have each discussed the importance of the idea of Wittgenstein's distinction between representations and standards of representation for literary theory, and I am indebted to their discussions. See Schalkwyk (1995) and Guetti (1993: 81–3).

representational. That is, it can embody reality by grounding a certain purchase on it, not by standing *in* for some other thing but by standing *for* it, in the sense that the narrative marks the moment of cultural production through which an aspect of our world is given form, shape, sense, and thus offers the lens through which we can see it. It thus becomes a standard for how that aspect of the word is understood, grasped, seen.

Now writers of literary works do not, presumably, see themselves as engaged in the construction of anything they should be inclined to call 'criteria' or 'standards of representation'. But it strikes me as plausible to think that the act of telling a story, of weaving a narrative, is a way of giving structure to a certain conception of human experience and circumstance—a way in which we 'are' in the world. And the point I am putting on offer is that the writers of many of our great works of literature offer us narratives that, as the saying goes, 'give order' to the world, if not by mirroring it—for fictions are hardly suited for that—then by being representative of various regions of it. A vision of fictions can perform this just as well as an image of something actual can—indeed better, since with fictions an author has the ability to manipulate the objects, to place them in just such a relationship, and actuality rarely behaves long enough to reveal itself in such an orderly fashion.

Though this will need further development, I hope one can see how it accounts for the sensation we often have of being able to see our world so clearly in a literary work while all the while knowing that we are witnessing nothing actual. Literature shows us reality, but at a level that is best described as foundational, placing before us those narratives that hold in place and in so doing structure our understanding of large regions of cultural reality. We see nothing actual in literature. But we do see something just as crucial from the worldly point of view: those stories in virtue of which expanses of human experience and circumstance are made visible to us. In this respect literary narratives enjoy a certain priority to representation, for their presentation of human practice can ground our sense of—rather than mirror—those practices.

If this is so, then we can begin to see how we can accept the 'fictionality' of literature—that a fiction is, after all, just that—yet maintain without contradiction that literature offers the reader a vital encounter with her world. What is barred from the idea of humanism on this account is an appreciative stance that casts literary content as *merely* fictional, that regards the frame of fiction as essentially incapable of holding in view anything more than a vision of creatures of pure fantasy. But it also asks us not to reawake the mimetic theory of literature to explain what this something more than *mere* fiction we find in literature might be. It asks us to see that calling (say) the Underground Man a fiction is to acknowledge that he represents no real thing. And it tells us that to go on to read *Notes from Underground* for reality is to recognize that we nevertheless can see in this creature of fiction—and literature more generally—those narratives in virtue of which we are able to narrate our own way in our world.

We read for this life not as the indirect humanist of Chapter 1 does, by looking away from the literary work and towards something external to it. It is precisely by exploring the interior of the literary work, by looking directly within it—*by reading it*—that we can come into contact with the life it has to show us. Thus the idea of humanism can be seen as resting upon a legitimate picture of literary appreciation. It is nothing but the words that run through a literary work that generate these narratives that are so important to a culture's ability to articulate to itself a sense of its world. If this is so, then we can begin to see that the sceptic's threat of literary isolationism has lost its teeth, for the reality we read for is a proper feature of literary content itself, in fact is in no significant respect distinguishable from it. The idea that reality is necessarily extra-textual and so beyond the purview of literary appreciation is thus misguided.

But still, one might say, what does it mean to say that we see in these fictions something 'real', that we see some aspect of the world *just as it is*? Let me conclude with a concrete critical example, one that I hope shall throw light on what it means to speak this way about our appreciation of a specific literary work.

I will consider a sort of experience that is not uncommon when reading literature. Say that in rereading *Othello* I realize that I have missed something, one of those instances of finding a new layer of complexity in a work read a number of times before. Although I very well know that Othello is the subject of Iago's angry discussion with Roderigo in the first act, I notice for the first time that never once is Othello mentioned by name. The first time Othello is explicitly referred to, it is not by his proper name but by his ethnicity: he is 'The Moor' (I. i. 40).[21] Iago is Othello's *ancient* and confidant—they know each other intimately—and if not for his anger we would expect him to call Othello by his proper name, and this I now see is subtly suggestive. A few lines later Roderigo adds colour to our picture of this nameless Moor by calling him 'thick-lips' (I. i. 66); and I begin to see a progression—in that vague way we become attuned to something taking shape when we read a literary work—that culminates in the first important scene of the tragedy. Iago decides to deliver his initial blow by telling Brabantio that his daughter has secretly married Othello. Again, not once is Othello's name used, and the words Iago uses reveal why:

Your heart is burst, you have lost half your soul; Even now, now, very now, an old Black ram is tupping your white ewe; arise, arise, Awake the snorting citizens with the bell, Or else the devil will make a grandsire of you. (I. i. 87–90)

Zounds, sir, you are one of those that will not service God, if the Devil bid you. Because we come to do you service, you think we are ruffians, you'll have your daughter covered with a Barbary horse; you'll have your nephews neigh to you; you'll have coursers for cousins, and gennets for germans. (I. i. 110–13)

I am one, sir, that come to tell you, your daughter, and the Moor, are now making the beast with two backs. (I. i. 115)

Iago's tactic in the above passages is to appeal to the crudest part of Brabantio: his gut-level sense of blood and purity, his racial instinct.

---

[21] All references are to the Ridley edition (1992).

Iago offers the image, so well crafted to pierce Brabantio's fatherly sense, of his daughter with an African animal, being 'tupped' by a black ram who will bring not proper grandchildren but cross-breeds into his family line.[22] There is neither a marriage nor a man depicted in Iago's words, just the image of a 'white ewe' copulating with a beast. (That Iago has skilfully chosen this tactic for Brabantio is attested to in the final act of the tragedy when Gratiano says: 'Poor Desdemona, I am glad thy father's dead; Thy match was mortal to him; and pure grief shore his old thread atwain' (v. ii. 205–6).) We have a word for this, even if Iago and Shakespeare did not. What is striking, and certainly brilliant, about the passage is how perfectly it captures what we call racism, how, we might say, *essentially* racist Iago's tactic is.

Now I am not, in emphasizing the work's references to Othello's blackness, asking that we understand the matter as though it is of a piece with race and blackness as it is addressed and understood in, say, twentieth-century American literature. Iago's strategy here is to dehumanize Othello by making him an outsider—an 'other', as it would be fashionable to say; and Othello's race is clearly the brush with which Iago paints this picture, regardless of what race and blackness might signify for Iago, Elizabethan audiences, or in the structure of the first act. Thus by 'racism' I am not suggesting that I have unearthed an ethical concept that Shakespeare is urging: race and ethnicity were for Shakespeare *dramatic* devices—consider also Aaron the Moor from *Titus Andronicus* and Shylock from *The Merchant of Venice*— and we should not expect him to have a moral interest in such a uniquely modern concern.

His drama does, however, *embody* this concept so perfectly that we find ourselves bearing witness to something that lies very near

---

[22] As far as I am aware, critics of *Othello*, at least since Coleridge (whose argument against reading Othello as a 'veritable Negro' is arguably itself a classic of racist reasoning), are generally agreed in this interpretation. The Shakespeare scholar Harold Bloom puts the point well, if grandiloquently, when he writes of Iago: 'the passed-over officer becomes the poet of street brawls, stabbings in the dark, disinformation, and above all else, the uncreation of Othello, the sparagmos of the great captain-general so that he can be returned to the original abyss, the chaos that Iago equates with the Moor's African origins' (Bloom 1998: 438).

the heart of what we understand this concept to *mean*, of what forms of human circumstance and interaction this concept has as its home. What we see is the gradual construction of a dehumanized picture of Othello. It begins with a reduction of his identity to what divides him from everyone else, his ethnicity; and from here on all the attendant expressions of racism are brought to life: the notion of the perversion of mixed blood, the idea that an act of love with a racial outsider amounts to sex with a subhuman, an animal, and so is a violation of one's body and family.[23] *This* is racism, we want to say. Let us see how we can make sense of it.

Now by 'this is racism' I do not mean to pick out some mimetic function of the work—say, the fact that Iago is acting and speaking as a real racist would. Trivially he is, or else we would not be inclined to call his tactic racist. But I mean something deeper than that the racism we see there *looks* like or imitates real racism. I want to say that it *is* racism. Nor—to dismiss another possibility—is my claim to be taken as saying that the text refers to or represents some extra-textual state of affairs. How would we explain this? Do we say that it represents a universal of some sort, that by 'this is racism' I mean to say that the text is a representation of some strange entity, perhaps Racism As Such? This is an unwanted idea, and in any case the sceptic, for his part, has shown us that the only legitimate application of notions of reference and representation to a work of literature is that of *fictional* reference and representation, to record how a novel describes an imaginatively created world. Lastly, I am not saying with my 'this is racism' that the text (or the scenes we have looked over) amounts to the claim that racism is thus and such sort of thing, as though my '*this*' functions to pick out a proposition

---

[23] Tellingly, Iago uses much the same racial strategy later in the tragedy against Othello himself. In giving him reasons to doubt Desdemona's faithfulness, he argues that it is in her nature to betray him: 'Ay, there's the point: as, to be bold with you,/Not to affect many proposed matches/Of her own clime, complexion, and degree/Whereto we see in all things nature tends-/Foh! one may smell in such a will most rank/Foul disproportion thoughts unnatural/But pardon me: I do not in position/Distinctly speak of her, though I may fear/Her will, recoiling to her better judgement/May fall to match you with her country forms/And happily repent' (III. iii. 231–41).

of some sort that is implied by the text. The text, as far as I can see, does not state either directly or indirectly a truth-valued proposition about race and the role it may play in love or culture. Again, the sceptic is right here: what the text describes, what it makes assertions and claims about, is the (fictional) world of its narrative line.

The sceptic is right that my 'this is racism' says something only about the content of the literary work, not some further extra-textual property it represents. But what he failed to see is that this does not imply an absence of reality. Whereas he thought isolationism followed from the admission that there is no extra-textual reference and representation, whereas he thought this claim implied a divide between the words of the text and the our-worldly, we now have a way of asserting a firm connection. The sceptic was not wrong, but blind to another possibility, one that we now have at our disposal.

When I claim of *Othello* that 'this is racism', my 'this' has, I suggest, the force of registering that the text speaks on the *criterial* level of what racism is. With slight but instructive bombast, we can say that, when Iago sets to turning Brabantio against Othello, he becomes our word for racism: so complete is Iago's expression of racism that we see exposed in his words the criteria for this feature of human reality. This is not to attribute any extraordinary powers to Shakespeare, except that power over words we know that writers of his endowment possess. To account for this we need only to point out what we have already seen, that Shakespeare's Iago, a creature of fiction though he may be, is nonetheless a fiction that draws together at such a level of detail all that goes into what we call 'racism' that there is no gap to be invoked between the text's expression of it and what this fixture of our culture *is*. Needless to say, the 'is' here is not the 'is' of the actual or the empirical. This 'is' rather marks the presence of the criterion of what racism *is*. My 'this is racism', then, does not record either the referential or the representational successes of *Othello*, for there is no success to be spoken of here. It records the success of its expression of racism, as an expression not of pure *Sinn*, but of that connection to our world that underlies what the sceptic took to be just 'mere' words. It is in this sense that we can claim that, if literature represents nothing real, we can see it as bringing into view our *standards* of representation, our criteria 'for what the world "is", without themselves being removed from that world'. [24]

If this is so, we do not need to look outside the literary work to explain the humanist connection. In fact, there is nothing outside the text that really matters to the humanist. We do not need to attempt to connect the literary with anything extra-literary to give support to humanism. We just look deeper into what is already in a literary work: our language. And the humanist can claim that, if we look deeply enough, we find that there is with it our world as well, not as a represented object but reality as it—to use Bernard Harrison's phrase—'permeates the thickness' of the language both we and the literary work of art speak.[25]

There is much more to be said about humanism, and the position I have developed here is only an introduction to a position I shall develop in the following chapters. In particular, we need an account of the epistemological significance of the connection the humanist has secured with reality, as well as an examination of the role interpretation plays in all of this. These are the topics to which I turn in the next two chapters. What I have done in this chapter is to wrestle humanism away from the grip of the sceptic's view of language. And what I hope we can now see is that it is possible to offer the humanist intuition a sturdy linguistic foundation. To

---

[24] Schalkwyk (1995: 288).
[25] In developing the argument of this chapter I am very indebted to the passage in which Harrison's phrase occurs. Harrison is, to my knowledge, the only contemporary literary aesthetician to try to find the connection to reality *in* the language of a literary work rather than in referential relations between literary work and world. As he argues: 'Literary language, the language of narrative fiction and poetry, is, root and branch, constitutive language. As such it is non-referential and it makes no statements... It is a language occupied solely with itself, *in a sense*. The mistake promoted by the Positivistic vision of language is to suppose that this sense can be absolute. Language is everywhere hopelessly infected with the extra-linguistic: the relationship between its signs runs ineluctably by way of the world. So there is, just as the critical humanist has always maintained, a strong connection between language and Reality; only it does not run by way of reference and truth. Rather, it permeates the thickness of the language we speak' (Harrison (1991: 51).

give life to the humanist intuition we need nothing—no suspicious metaphysical object, no mysterious act of squeezing an extra-textual representation out of a textual form that trades in fictional reference, no comparison between the world of the text and our world—except the language than runs through the literary work of art.

3

Beyond Truth and Triviality

The previous chapter offered a foundation to humanism by undoing the sceptic's isolationist view of literary language. In taking from the sceptic his isolationist conclusion, in effect forcing him to default on his scepticism—without isolationism there is no pressing sceptical stance—we saw that nothing in the idea of the literary implies the incoherence of humanism, nothing, that is, except a misguided picture of the nature of language. What the humanist has been looking for, and what he appears to have found, is a way of speaking about the presence of reality in literature that is compatible with literature's explicit lack of worldly representation and reference.

Literature is an exclusively linguistic affair, a sort of convening of the words of our language with no pretence to using these words to mirror the objects with which they are associated in their standard descriptive usage. But the mistake, an understandable but dangerous one, is to hear this as implying a loss of reality. The error lies in thinking that there is no alternative, that we have either worldly reference or linguistic self-reference, a depiction of the actual world or words that speak of nothing but themselves. We give linguistic plausibility to humanism by arguing that literature exposes reality not by way of extra-textual representation. Literature reveals the world by bringing to light our criterial relation with reality, our standards of representation. In this way we can reconcile the idea that literature speaks in independence from the stirrings of extra-textual reality with the seemingly incompatible idea that the literary work of art can put us into intimate contact with our world.

But, while we have won the right to speak like a humanist, we nevertheless have not yet learned quite *how* to speak like a humanist. The way in which we saw that we can give sense to the basic humanist claim may collapse the wall the sceptic placed around the literary work, but as a statement about how literature can reveal reality it is in one very important respect incomplete.

We might put the problem in the following way. We have found a connection stronger than humanism's traditional use of the notion of mimetic resemblance (so much is implied by the idea that we see the world rather than a mimetic duplication of it in literature).[1] We have a connection stronger than verisimilitude. But we do not yet have *veritas*, an understanding of the intellectual value of the presentation of the our-worldly in literature. We have a way of speaking about the possibility of seeing reality in literature, but the humanist needs this seeing to be significant, not only a vision of reality but an illumination of it. In short, we need an account of the *cognitive* value of the presentation of reality literature can offer.

Whatever 'cognitive' may mean in its various technical uses, as I will use the term here (and as it is generally used in the literature on aesthetics), it has the sense of asking whether literature can be seen as in some significant respect *informative* of extra-textual reality. It asks whether literature can declare to the reader something about the way her world is, whether this presentation of the world the humanist has shown literature capable of can in any way be described as a form of *cognitive* presentation. Without this further step, one opens oneself up to the charge that her theory is better described as just '*anti* anti-humanism'[2] rather than a genuine humanistic theory: an

---

[1] A notion perhaps most notably used in Aristotelian varieties of humanism. We see the roots of 'mimetic' humanism in the famous line of the *Poetics* at 51^{b}27: 'a "writer" [*poises*] must be a composer of plots rather than verse, insofar as he is writer according to representation [*mimesis*], and represents actions.' The humanistic force of this claim is found a few lines latter in the *Poetics* (51^{a}38–40), when Aristotle argues that there is a 'universal' element in mimesis, though there is tremendous variation in opinion as to what Aristotle means by 'universal' (*katholou*) here.

[2] A charge Stanley Bates (1998) brings against Lamarque and Olsen's so-called no-truth theory of humanism.

argument that silences the sceptic who claims that literature has nothing to do with reality, but not a claim to the effect that literature actually has something interesting to show us about reality. We may see the world in literature, but, if literature cannot offer a cognitively interesting engagement with reality, it is hard to see why it is worth learning how to speak like a humanist, why one should care about literature's ability to present reality to us.

At this point all we have is a model for describing how we can see our world directly in the literary-fictive use of language. This is important, of course, for it offers humanism a foundation. But it is just that, a foundation; and in attempting to build upon it a number of challenges present themselves. The question of the cognitive value of literature is one of the central debates in literary aesthetics, and so one now enters a discussion that brings with it its own set of problems.

There is a very simple and well-known way of formulating the problem as it is most threatening to a defence of humanism. It is a problem that is most notoriously associated with mimetic theories of art—as Plato saw and duly ridiculed the idea that art is cognitively valuable—and is captured well by Arthur Danto:

[Socrates] spoke of art as a mirror held up to nature . . . Socrates saw mirrors as but reflecting what we can already see; so art, insofar as mirror-like, yields idle accurate duplications of the appearances of things, and is of no cognitive benefit whatsoever.[3]

The reason the mimetic theory makes art cognitively trivial is not specific to the fact that it casts art as 'mirror-like'. It is because it invites a much more general difficulty. Art, on the mimetic model, turns out to be cognitively trivial because it can do nothing more than bring before us a world with which we are already very much acquainted. It may hold our world up for view, but it adds nothing to our understanding of it.

We might call it the problem of *cognitive familiarity*, and the sceptic claims that he can show us that it infects the theory of

---

[3] Danto (1964: 571).

humanism I am proposing. The sceptic charges that all the humanist is entitled to claim is that the strongest cognitive relation we have to literature is that we see in it aspects of our world knowledge of which we already possess. The sceptic grants that we see—to switch from racism to a much more familiar aspect of the tragedy—jealousy just as it is when we read *Othello*, and thus for the other fixtures of our world given expression in literary works. But surely, he says, we knew what jealousy was long before reading or viewing this tragedy. Indeed, the sceptic reasonably claims, my very ability to identify Othello as jealous suggests that this literary work *presupposes* rather than *imparts* knowledge of this bit of human reality; if not, my ability to *recognize* Othello as jealous would be quite mysterious. At the very least, the sceptic charges, nothing hitherto said permits us to claim otherwise.

Even if the vision of human reality we find in literature is 'deep', even if it occurs somewhere near the heart of what (say) jealousy or suffering or anger *is*, the sceptic correctly points out that this only rescues us from the grips of isolationism. But it brings us nowhere near a vindication of the idea that literature might actually offer cognitive rewards to the careful reader. Literature may hold up reality for appreciation, the sceptic says. But, much like an expertly crafted map of a region we already know well, the vision of reality found in literary works is without cognitive consequence. Literature's presentation of our world may be brilliant as a feat of aesthetic accomplishment, but it is ultimately a view of quite familiar territory.

The sceptic gives up his charge of literary isolationism and begins to reinvent himself as the anti-cognitivist sceptic. He accepts that the humanist has provided an alternative to the picture of literary language that leads to isolationism. But he argues that there is a dubious chance that one can show that literature's presentation of reality can in any way be informative of reality. Thus the sceptic modifies his position and sets forth this revised sceptical charge: *literature may not be isolated from the world but the connection it offers to the world is cognitively trivial.*

The sceptic challenges us to show that literature does *anything* in its presentation of our world that could offer a reason for even treating it as engaged in the pursuit of knowledge and similar sorts of cognitive illumination He asks us to show that literature can offer *any* understanding of the world, of whatever sort. If the humanist can show this, he would then open the door to any number of precise species of cognitive rewards: this novel is cognitively valuable because it shows us some previously undocumented feature of human experience, that novel because it confirms our ancient and entrenched beliefs, this novel because it shocks a certain picture of reality, that novel because it secures it, and so on. But first we must meet this much more basic condition, and this is what the sceptic claims we cannot do.

What we will see is that the sceptic has little difficulty taking from the humanist two terms traditionally associated with cognitive value: truth and knowledge. The task will then become one of showing that the humanist's forfeiture of these notions does not imply that literature is cognitively trivial. There may seem to be an intolerable tension in this claim—what is a cognitive value without truth and knowledge?—but what I will argue is that there is a reasonable and indeed powerful alternative. I hope to show that the foundation secured in the last chapter can be developed in such a way that we can see literature as offering a different sort of intellectual reward, one that, while not consisting in the deliverance of worldly truth and knowledged, nevertheless allows us to see that literature can offer a vital cognitive engagement with reality.

3.1. TEXTS *AS* TRUTHS?

We are looking for a way to make sense of the idea that literature can offer cognitive rewards to the careful reader. The traditional, and most obvious, way of approaching the issue is to ask whether it offers knowledge of extra-textual reality by attempting to lead the reader to truths about the way the world is. But, as I will argue here, this route is unavailable to the humanist. The history of the philosophy of literature and literary theory provides the sceptic with a wide range of arguments that show that neither of these terms has any interesting literary application, and here I want to bring the reasons for this into full view. After the first two chapters we are already familiar with the reasons why literature and truth make for frigid bedfellows, so the arguments the sceptic gives here against the idea of (as it is often called) 'knowledge *through* literature' will neither come as much of a surprise nor require immense elaboration. What I will do here is investigate a small but important area of the debate that the arguments of the previous chapters have not touched on.

Before beginning, we need to establish exactly where our humanist finds himself in this debate. We have been exploring the possibility of a strong internal connection between literature and reality. But we found that humanism runs into the problem of cognitive familiarity, for the position thus far developed offers no obvious way of going beyond the notion that, for some worldly ϕ we find in literature, literature assumes, rather than transmits, knowledge of what ϕ is.

Let us agree that the direct route out of this impasse, one that would allow the humanist to introduce a notion of literature as a conveyer of worldly truth and knowledge, would be to find a way to show that, in presenting some fixture of social and cultural reality to view—a sort of presentation of which the humanist can now claim literature to be capable of—literature is also able to *tell* us something about it (perhaps offer a deeper understanding of its character, perhaps inform us of some hidden corner of its nature, and so on). This is to ask something as simple as it is intuitive. It is to query whether *Othello* might be able to reveal something about *what jealousy is* in presenting jealousy to view. If *Notes from Underground* brings suffering to our attention, we could show literature to be capable of offering knowledge of the world if we can find a way to treat the text as also attempting to inform us about some aspect of the nature of suffering.[4] We are not asking whether literature might trade in justified true belief or lay bare the universal nature of things, should we be tempted to hear particularly technical epistemological or metaphysical issues invited by this question. It will be enough for us to find that literature might try to tell us something—*anything*—about the nature of those aspects of our world it brings to view, and for the present we will not require anything more of it.[5]

This requirement is about as minimal as they come, and what we will see here is that it is still impossible to meet. To show this, let me introduce someone I will call the *truth-seeking* humanist: the humanist who believes that literature can offer worldly knowledge of the sort just described. We will see that the truth-seeking humanist is misguided, but, like the indirect humanist of Chapter 1, his mistake tells us something important about literature, and through his error we will see where we must go if we are to find a way to answer the sceptic. A few brief examples will suffice to bring to view what the truth-seeking humanist has in mind.

Othello, the truth-seeking humanist brings to our attention, does not merely present jealousy to view, as though 'jealousy' sits in the text as an immobile, granite-like presence. Its presence is better understood as a fluid that runs through, and in so doing is given shape by, the events of the tragedy. At the moment Othello takes Desdemona's life we have a vision of jealousy greatly more complex than we find when Iago first sets to stirring this emotion in Othello. And the truth-seeking humanist suggests that, through its dramatic presentation of jealousy, *Othello* yields what looks to be a genuine candidate for a *claim* about what jealousy is, that (let us agree for the sake of argument) 'jealousy is a rage that can destroy what one holds most dear'. Likewise, *Medea* presents not just 'anger'

---

[4] As it is often called, 'propositional' or 'discursive' knowledge, which would be to ask whether literature can make claims of the basic 'ϕ is thus and such' a sort of thing (that 'jealousy is thus and such', etc.).

[5] See Gaut (in Levinson 2003; in Kieran 2006) for very clear and insightful overviews of the different epistemological issues at play in this debate.

to view but what looks very like an assertion about what anger is. Through the progression of dramatic events, *Medea* offers a presentation of anger that yields the claim—as the Greek Stoic Chrysippus said we learn from this tragedy—that 'anger is a passion that destroys reason and judgment'.[6] Perhaps we might even see the entirety of *Anna Karenina* as functioning to lead us to the truth of the sentence with which Tolstoy begins the novel: 'All happy families are alike but an unhappy family is unhappy after its own fashion.'

Consider all that Martha Nussbaum claims *Hecuba* can show us:

> I have said that this tragedy *shows* us a case of solid character and shows us that, under certain circumstances, even this cannot escape defilement. It also has *shown* us that even the good character who has not suffered any actual damage or betrayal lives always with the risk of these events... in this sense nothing human is ever *worthy* of trust: there are no guarantees at all, short of revenge or death.[7]

At first glance this way of talking about literary texts might strike us as perfectly legitimate, if only owing to how familiar a note it should sound to anyone who has ever read a book review. And notice that Nussbaum's account of *Hecuba* is teeming with claims to genuine knowledge acquisition. *Hecuba* does not just tell us that 'nothing human is ever worthy of trust'; *it shows us this!* This is a strong claim indeed, and of precisely the sort the truth-seeking humanist wants. If literary texts can in fact show us what Nussbaum claims *Hecuba* can show us, a viable theory of literary knowledge cannot be very far away.

How might the truth-seeking humanist elicit from these general observations a way of seeing literature as proffering genuine *claims* about the way the world is? He has an interesting alternative at his disposal, one that suggests a way of getting round all the arguments for the independence of literature from truth canvassed earlier. We have known since the sceptic's recital that the individual sentences

---

[6] See Gill (1983) for a discussion of this.   [7] Nussbaum (1986: 419).

of a text do not make truth claims by referring, representing, or otherwise describing the world. The sentences of a work of fiction are 'beyond' truth valuation in this sense: they are not asserted of the world, thus they cannot be the bridge by which the truth-seeking humanist unites a literary work with truths about the way our world is. But the truth-seeking humanist has an unplayed card. He can claim that, while the individual sentences of the literary text state no truths, we can take the *text as a whole* as generating a claim about the way the world is. The truth-seeking humanist ignores the referential and representational properties of the text's sentences taken individually—we already know the connection to reality cannot lie here—and instead asks what sort of bridge to reality we might find if we investigate the literary work taken as a whole.

Nothing about the world is revealed or illuminated when we ask what the individual sentences of the text are about: they are about fictions or make claims that operate to qualify[8] the fictional world of the text. But, if we take the text as a whole, which can bear properties its individual sentences cannot,[9] we have a route to worldly truth left untouched by the sceptical arguments canvassed earlier. At the very least, we have a way of conceiving how a literary text might generate statements about the nature of human reality when none of its individual sentences speaks of the actual, and this is enough for the truth-seeking humanist to build on.[10]

---

[8] This condition is needed to make allowances for the 'reflective' statements we find in literature (say when Iago says of jealousy that it is 'the green-eyed monster'), which are not in any straightforward way descriptions of proper fictional objects or states of affairs.

[9] This would be one way of emphasizing that a literary text is a *work*, a vehicle of meaning over and above the 'meanings' of the individual sentences of which it is composed. (Think, if an analogy is needed, of a piece of music: *Rhapsody in Blue* as a work bears properties and values—conveys impressions and emotions—its various notes do not.) I discuss this in detail in the next chapter.

[10] This leaves aside poststructuralist arguments to the effect that a literary text does not generate *a* determinate statement at all. Since the position I am describing here will be shown to be untenable in any case, I hope anyone with a particular interest in this question will forgive my not going into what would be very involved discussion.

The truth-seeking humanist has brought to our attention what is commonly called the *thematic* level of literature.[11] This level of a literary work, he claims, offers a way of conceiving how a literary work might shape and structure our understanding of the bits of our world we find in a text such that we can see a literary work as attempting to say something about the nature of these aspects of our world. At what we might call the *fictional* level of interpretation, the level at which we analyse the content of the individual sentences of the literary text, we find only reports on the 'truths' that hold in a fictional world (such as when Othello says of himself that he 'loved not wisely, but too well'). But, at the thematic level, the level at which the action of the narrative line forges a distinct conception of (broadly put) life, we find a way of conceiving how a work of literature can generate a statement about the real world (as we might say that we see in Othello's succumbing to Iago's falsification of Desdemona a general statement to the effect that 'jealousy thrives on the weakness of trust').[12]

The truth-seeking humanist argues that he has given us a way to see a literary work as a chain of interpretation, of which the individual dramatic events are links and through which a claim is developed, a point pursued, until a structured insight is yielded. If this is so, it appears that the truth-seeking humanist can claim that a literary work can be *informative* of the aspects of human reality it presents to view. The content of a thematic statement is uncontaminated by fictional reference and thus by that which has blocked the humanist from invoking the notion of truth in our

---

[11] See Pocci, in Gibson, Huemer, and Pocci (2007), for an excellent discussion of the nature of literary themes and thematic criticism.

[12] It is sometimes argued that what we commonly refer to as a 'theme' requires finer distinction, otherwise we have trouble gracefully distinguishing the conceptual subject of a novel, say romantic love, and the specific 'vision' of this it pursues, say romantic love as a blind passion. Beardsley argues, for example, that we might distinguish *theme* from *thesis*, and use the notion of 'theme', roughly put, to specify the conceptual subject and 'thesis' the particular conceptualization of it given in the literary work. See Beardsley (1981: 402–11. My generic use of the term 'theme', I hope, suffices for the general point I am pursuing here.

past discussions. Thus the truth-seeking humanist claims that he has made reasonable the idea that literature can advance truths about the world in a structured manner, using the text as a whole as the vehicle of cognitive acquisition. For we have a way of seeing literary texts as fashioning the aspects of the our-worldly they present to view into an insight into their nature. We have a way of seeing how *Othello* does something more than merely present jealousy to view. By working the concept of jealousy through the various events of the tragedy, *Othello* advances claims about *what jealousy is*.

There is an initial plausibility to this idea that a literary work, in offering a thematic interpretation of human reality, reveals something about it (my positive argument for humanism at the end of the chapter will attempt to salvage what is right in this idea). The sceptic grants that everything the truth-seeking humanist has said *sounds* right. But he argues that something is amiss, a slight but damaging confusion in the way the truth-seeking humanist understands the terms he is using. The sceptic admits—he would be unreasonable not to—that the thematic level of appreciation builds some sort of bridge between our world and a fictional world. Descriptions of the theme of a literary text pick out interpretations of our most significant practices and experiences, and this no doubt blows worldly relevance into the happenings of the fictional world of a literary work. What sounds right in the truth-seeking humanist's argument is his insistence that the thematic level of literature offers conceptualizations of experience that speak to our sense of the significance of these experiences (it appeals, to state a platitude, to what we care about). But he goes astray in thinking that the thematic dimension of literary works can be analysed in the vocabulary of truth and knowledge acquisition.

The initial difficulty lies in the work the truth-seeking humanist wants thematic statements to do. If we think carefully for a few moments, it becomes very difficult to see what would entitle us to treat thematic statements as having 'assertive' force, as bona fide claims made about the way our world is. A literary work yields a thematic statement in so far as it allows us to 'read off' the dramatic events of a story a certain conceptual structure, a sense of something general being given expression in the particular fictional happenings of the work. So, when we ask what supports our ascription of a thematic statement to a literary work, we point to a succession of events in the narrative line. The basic problem, of course, is that this would appear to put us into contact with plot occurrences rather than points of entry into reality.

When we explain the extension of a thematic statement, we are lead not to the world but to a bond of fictional characters and events, and so we are faced with the fact that a thematic statement 'says' nothing more than that thus and such a concept unifies or otherwise finds expression in the dramatic structure of a literary narrative. In other words, the content of a thematic statement has not epistemological but literary-critical import: it informs us of the conceptual structure of the literary work and not the nature of our world. Nothing in this, the sceptic argues, entitles us to invoke the notion of truth, to treat literature as trying to proffer knowledge of extra-literary reality.

In this respect the sceptic charges that the truth-seeking humanist has not offered us a way of understanding how we might squeeze a claim with genuine assertive force out of a thematic statement. For there is nothing in our understanding of the logic of the generation of thematic statements that permits us to treat these statements as at all said of extra-textual reality. These (putative) statements yielded by a literary work 'taken whole' are not genuine statements about extra-textual reality: they apply only to the structure of the literary text and in no obvious way reach out of it and lay claim to the way the world is. As Lamarque and Olsen put it:

Literary appreciation is concerned with the application of a set of thematic concepts to a particular work. It is not concerned with any further reality to which these concepts might be applied in their other uses. Appreciation, through interpretation, mediates the connection between the work and thematic concepts; but it does no more. Literature offers its own alternative realm of application. It offers an imaginative rather than discursive interpretation of the concepts. And this possibility of applying thematic concepts in literary appreciation makes no direct contribution to philosophical or theological insight, nor is it tied to any such aim. It constitutes its own form of insight, its own kind of interpretation of concepts. The nature of this insight can be analysed by giving a description of how thematic concepts are attached to literary works. But one can do nothing further to throw light on it.[13]

The truth-seeking humanist is right to think that by regarding theme as a potential mouthpiece of worldly truth we can get around the problem posed by the sceptic in Chapter 1—namely, that the descriptions of a literary text put us into contact only with a fictional world. But what we are beginning to see is that the literary work itself offers us nothing on which to base a claim to the effect that literature tries to send these thematic statements out into reality, and so we find that it offers no way of escaping the sceptic's charge of cognitive triviality.

There is a very simple way of putting this. We might call it the problem of *unclaimed truths*. Now, need it be mentioned, of course a thematic statement may be true of the world, in the dull sense that any string of words with propositional content bears a truth value. But its truth is unclaimed by the text, for the text does not assert these thematic statements *of* reality. So, while it may be true of both *Othello's* world and ours that 'jealousy destroys what one holds most dear', *Othello* does nothing to attempt to inform us of the worldly truth of this. While the thematic statements we elicit from a literary work may be true of reality, they are not claimed *of* reality *by* the literary work. They are said of, and function to inform us about, the world of the literary work, 'facts' about its narrative line. So we lose the idea that thematic statements provide a reason for conceiving literature as trying to *tell* us about the world. The truth-seeking humanist, in this respect, finds himself snared in the sceptic's old traps: world-constructing texts such as works of literary fiction have only an incidental and contingent relation to worldly truth.

---

[13] Lamarque and Olsen (1994: 408–9).

There is another argument against the possibility of treating literature as a provider of worldly knowledge, one so often stated that there is hardly an original word for the sceptic to add to it. As Gordon Graham puts it:

> An important difference remains between a work of art and a work of inquiry, namely that the latter has a structure of reasoning by which it moves from premise to conclusion, whereas the former does not. History, science, and philosophy are disciplines, organized systems of knowledge, not merely of collections of isolated facts or propositions. Intellectual inquiry does not just confront the mind with facts or hypothesis, but *directs* it through a progression of thought, and it is this capacity which allows us to call these modes *of understanding*. In contrast, it seems that the best art can do is to present a point of view. Even writers sympathetic to the idea of truth in art have generally supposed that art merely expresses truth, not that it argues for it. If it does not argue for it, then it cannot be said to properly *show* it.[14]

And Lamarque and Olsen are again worth quoting here:

> If literary works are construed as having the constitutive aim of advancing truths about human concerns by means of general propositions implicitly or explicitly contained in them, then one should expect to find some kind of supporting argument... however, there are no such arguments or debates either in the literary work, or in literary criticism. Literary works cannot therefore be construed as one among other discourses with the intention of stating truths.[15]

When we find arguments of this sort, we should read them as drawing our attention to something more than the tedious point that literature does not establish truths about the world by way of rigid proofs and justifications, which we surely already knew. The interesting problem we see alluded to here is not epistemological but *classificatory*, a matter of whether we would group literature with

---

[14] Graham (1995: 196). Graham, it should be noted, is not an anti-cognitivist. Later in this article he argues that literature, while not presenting proper truths, does 'enhance' our understanding of reality by imaginatively illuminating experience.

[15] Lamarque and Olsen (1994: 368).

those disciplines and discourse forms that we take to attempt to offer knowledge. As Lamarque and Olsen put it, it is a question of whether we find anything *in* literary works that would entitle us to claim that literature even has the *intention* of stating truths, that it even feigns to present itself as a player in the pursuit of worldly knowledge.

It is built into our idea of a knowledge-pursuing discipline—say, history, science, or philosophy—that at the very least it offers *reasons* for taking its claims to be true of the world, that is has some argumentative structure, however minimal, that provides an incentive for believing that a text has set its sights on showing us something about the world.[16] Of course, the presence of an argumentative structure does not *secure* knowledge, as though we think that any text with an argumentative structure, just in virtue of possessing this structure, is therefore a reliable messenger of worldly truth. In fact it may even be the case that we do not think that our most prized scientific and philosophical works 'really' offer truth: we can read Newton without being Newtonians and Plato without giving any credence to Platonism. But, the sceptic reasonably points out, we do at least find some minimal argumentative or reason-giving structure, and this would appear to be what entitles us to classify a text as of the sort that engages in an enquiry into the way the world is, regardless of whether it is successful or insolvent in its attempt.

Without the presence of at least some sort of argumentative structure, it is very unclear what would invite us to treat a textual (or discourse) form as attempting to inform us about the world, what would even solicit the notion of knowledge pursuit. Even in the case of the various thought experiments and allegories we

---

[16] This leaves aside the question of what might constitute the presence of an argumentative structure. The answer to this question will vary from discipline to discipline, conservative to liberal. The challenge, obviously, is to find *anything* that resembles one in literature, and this way of putting it casts the net wide enough to touch on any intuitive notion of what counts as an argumentative structure or procedure of reason-giving.

find in science and philosophy—which, like literature, describe fictional scenarios—we find the presentation of a premiss, a chain of reasoning, *something* in virtue of which we take the fictions described to be attempting to lead us towards a worldly truth. When we examine literature, need we even point this out, we find plot occurrences rather than premisses, dramatic events rather than supporting evidence, aesthetic feats rather than philosophical analysis. Now it is no surprise that we do not find a structure of argumentation in literature. But the obvious question is, what then is there in a literary work that would call on us to treat it as attempting to offer truths about the world? If literature functioned to pursue worldly truths, it would appear that it would have a status not much more respectable than that of texts that trade in groundless declaration and bald pronouncement—probably worse, since, even in the most vacant works of new age cabalism and paranoid conspiratorial politics, we find at least an illusion of reason-giving or a hoax of argumentation. But, the sceptic argues, the very fact that literature does not have this status brings home the fact that literature is independent of argumentative forms of writing rather than just a poor participant in the same search for truth.

We can, of course, *use* a literary text in the pursuit of knowledge, a fact we have known since we examined the indirect humanist of Section 1.1. If we allow ourselves to blow argumentation into the literary work, we will find that it offers endless ways of coming to know reality. Through our philosophical reflections on the world of *Othello,* we can no doubt come into possession of truths about our own world, an achievement that requires nothing more than extracting the thematic statements we find there from their literary context and scrutinizing them as positions in a philosophical debate. But unfortunately this is of no help to the humanist. While manœuvres such as this may aid in our pursuit of knowledge, should we take this step we will lose the literary work and thus the very thing the humanist is trying to explain. It requires that we sever the stances, themes, and perspectives we find in a work from their literary context and treat them as free-floating propositions, asking what they might tell us about reality if we disregard their place and function in the text and instead treat them as isolated assertions about the way the world is.

The entire humanist enterprise is one of attempting to identify a humanistic *literary* value, some property *in* the text that is at once also revelatory of the worldly. This is what I earlier called the 'textual constraint' (see Section 1.2). The humanist is constrained to describe how literature presents the world as a form of *literary* presentation, as a proper feature of literary content. Otherwise his theory fails to be a theory of literature and reveals itself to be just an explanation of what we can do with a literary work if we steal bits and pieces of it for use as fodder for non-literary discussions. To make such a move is in effect to abandon the idea that a literary work *itself* can inform us about the way the world is, and at this point it ceases to be relevant to a defence of literary humanism.

This reveals why claims such as Peter Kivy's, however ingenious, cannot offer the humanist much help:

Now if one thinks, as I do, that part of the reader's literary appreciation consists in confirming and disconfirming for himself the general thematic statements he perceives in the fictional works he reads, sometimes unaided, sometimes through the help of literary critics, one will see why it is quite compatible with the Propositional Theory [of learning from literature] that such confirmation and disconfirmation are part of *appreciation*, and appreciation is the job, if I may so put it, of the reader, not the critic *qua* critic. The critic's job, *qua* critic, is, among other things, to make available to the reader whatever hypothesis the fictional work may, directly or indirectly, propose. It is the reader's job to appreciate them, in part by confirming or disconfirming them for himself.[17]

This seems to me tantamount to claiming that, if a literary work is to have cognitive value, it is because we *convert* a literary theme into a philosophical claim. We can do this, of course, should we feel so inclined. But, if we do, I fear we will find ourselves engaged in philosophical rather than literary appreciation, and thus that what

[17] Kivy (1997: 125).

we glean from this act of conversion will shed light on very much the wrong thing: on how *philosophical* rather than *literary* activity can bear cognitive value. We do not in any literal sense find these 'hypotheses' in literary works, and thus our appreciation of these hypotheses, though occasioned by our encounters with the literary, cannot itself be properly literary. When we convert a theme into the form of a hypothesis (or proposition), we are already at one remove from the work; and when we begin scrutinizing this hypothesis for truth, we soon find ourselves at a second. And it seems clear that the labour put into forging the connection to truth is performed almost entirely by the reader rather than the work, and thus we face the old problems. We have known since Chapter 1 that it is not a good idea to try to support humanism by finding some way to make literature (or literary appreciation) *mimic* philosophy (or, even less likely, science). It is a way of getting what we want too cheaply, assuming, as it does, that we must make literature piggyback on non-literary activities and pursuits if we are to show it to have cognitive value.

The upshot of all this is that, while it may be true that through our philosophical reflections on literary content we can erect positions that make a claim about the way the world is, when we examine these derived positions we are no longer really talking about literature. We quickly find that these derived 'positions' and 'claims' are aesthetically impure, literarily heretical, for they in no way can stand in substitution for the proper object of literary investigation, the work itself. To think otherwise is to fail to take seriously, one might say, the 'literature' we find in literary works, which is a rather unpardonable sin if our intention is to say something about the nature of our engagement with a novel, play, or poem. To move from literary work to worldly truth is to step away from that to which we want to be brought closer. This step is alluring but unfortunately unavailable to the humanist. As Terrence Diffey puts it:

To learn from a work of art, that is, to move from what is shown in the world of the work to an assertion that obtains in the world, requires a refusal of the aesthetic stance... It constitutes a further move, and out of the work, notwithstanding Derridean scepticism about the impossibility of getting out of a text and into something else, to assert of the text, 'and this is how it is'.[18]

It is difficult to see what more can be added to the sceptic's case. The arguments offered in the previous chapters force us to accept that we cannot take the sentences of a literary text as stating truths, and we now have seen that there is no promise in a retreat to the idea that we can take a literary work as a whole as yielding truths about the world. And so the sceptic concludes that literature is cognitively trivial. It does not offer truths about the world, *for it does not even attempt to tell us about the way the world is*. Thus literature cannot be a vehicle of worldly knowledge. The cognition-qua-knowledge paradigm, so central to the understanding of how our other core disciplines such as science and philosophy have cognitive value, is inapplicable to literature.

3.2. MERE KNOWLEDGE

The truth-seeking humanist has brought us no further ahead, and so we are no closer to finding a way round the problem of cognitive familiarity. The sceptic, recall, began by telling us that the foundation for humanism developed in the previous chapter runs into the problem of cognitive familiarity by inviting the argument that literature assumes rather than imparts knowledge of the world. And we can see that he is right, at least in so far as his anti-cognitivist arguments appear to make impossible the move to the idea that literature might actually be able to tell us something about the nature of reality. So, if it is true that *Othello* presents jealousy to view, the work nevertheless does not, cannot, offer any knowledge of *what jealousy is* in this act of literary presentation. And we can say the same of any of the aspects of our world we find given expression in

[18] Diffey (1995: 208–9).

literature. Literature may hold reality up for view; but the sceptic argues that, when it does, it offers it as an aesthetic object, used to texture the interior of the literary artwork, and not as a route to further worldly knowledge.

So what can the humanist do? We might begin by asking ourselves whether there is not something unsatisfying with the way both the truth-seeking humanist and the anti-cognitivist sceptic carry out the debate. We feel, or so our humanist does, swindled, as though we have just seen a question of genuine significance proposed and settled in terms in which it was probably never meant to be discussed (perhaps not unlike when we argue with someone who scrutinizes the belief in morality by asking whether its rules are 'verifiable' or its propositions 'empirical': we feel cheated in being forced to settle the question on this front, with these notions determining the fate of our belief in one of our fundamental areas of concern). Nothing is terribly surprising in the idea that literature does not 'state' truths about reality. Indeed there is a slight prick of embarrassment in stating this point that is transparent to many of us. Yet, while it may be true that literature cannot be 'cognitive' in the way the sceptic has shown it cannot be, we probably also think that there is something amiss in approaching the issue as both the truth-seeking humanist and sceptic do. We might feel forced to let them carry out the debate in these terms because it can seem that we must if we want to do justice to the idea—one most of us would not lose lightly—that literary experience is cognitive. But I think that we also find that we are not particularly surprised to learn that this route is unavailable. And this is the source of our frustration, for it is unclear where to go from here.

I would even suggest that we do think, though in a sense still unsettled, that literature ultimately does just trade in the familiar. Othello, after all, is only a jealous husband, Anna just a dejected lover. On a moment's reflection we find that most of the candidates for truths we thought we might find in literature are not especially revealing or insightful. Grandiloquence aside, 'jealousy can destroy what one holds most dear' and 'anger undoes reason' are 'truths'

I would think many of us would be ashamed to be ignorant of before our reading of *Othello* and *Medea*. Once stripped of their fine wording, they actually say something quite mundane, assuming as I am that none of us is shocked to find that jealousy can bring out the savage in us, anger the lunatic.

In fact, there would be something seriously amiss with a theory of humanism that casts literature as having cognitive value only for those of us with cognitive *defects*—for those of us in possession of, as it is sometimes called, 'culpable ignorance'—and this is what the truth-seeking humanist fails to see. Even if we could learn these truths from literature, we would not much cherish literature on account of it. It would suggest that literature has humanistic value because it can educate the oblivious among us, and I doubt one would be inclined to place the literary on a very high intellectual pedestal for this reason. As steadfastly as we might wish to cling to the notion that literature offers cognitive rewards, we should not find so counter-intuitive the claim that in literary experience we do not come into contact (for the first time, as it were) with new corners of reality so much as we find ourselves drawn to those we already inhabit and with which we are already familiar: the everyday realm of emotion, morality, sexuality, selfhood, and so on.

What I want to propose is that there is no tension here, that we can accept the sceptic's argument without being a turncoat to the humanist. The sceptic, let us agree for now at least, is right to say that literature trades in the familiar. Apart from the fact that we have no ground on which to assert the contrary, it is not an idea we should find particularly alien to common ways of thinking about literature. What the sceptic has wrong is that he believes that he has settled the matter, that this admission forces us to give up the search for the cognitive value of literature. It forces us to give up the idea that literature is in the business of offering worldly truth and knowledge. But the humanist, I will argue, can accept this without injury to his intuition.

There is another way of approaching the issue, a route unnoticed in both the truth-seeking humanist's and the sceptic's way of framing the problem. Rather than imparting truths, we might try to see the cognitive dimension of literature as consisting in literature's ability to operate upon the truths we already possess. We ask whether literature might have the ability to work upon the familiar such that we can see its cognitive power as consisting in how it can exploit our worldly knowledge rather than be a vehicle of it. There is, I want to show, a cognitive act that goes beyond knowledge as the sceptic and truth-seeking humanist conceive it, a form of understanding that literature is especially able to offer.[19]

What we need is a cognitive model on which to base this claim. In developing one, I will make use of Stanley Cavell's distinction between knowing and acknowledging.[20] The distinction is quite simple, and, if we draw out its implications, we can begin to find a way of describing the cognitive value of literature that points up an alternative to the sceptic's and truth-seeking humanist's search for worldly knowledge. I should mention, to the extent these things require mentioning, that I do not take what I say here to be straightforward Cavellian exegesis. Cavell uses this distinction to illuminate topics ranging from scepticism and Shakespeare interpretation to Hollywood cinema and moral perfectionism, and I do not pretend here to offer a systematic interpretation of Cavell's lithe use of the concept of acknowledgement in his work. What I do here is borrow the distinction and let the humanist develop it as he wishes.

---

[19] In recent years there has been a steady proliferation of philosophers who have noticed that art has an important power to offer forms of insight that in no obvious way rest upon the proffering of standard sorts of knowledge. Noël Carroll has argued that the ethical value of art is a matter not of its offering a body of moral knowledge but of its capacity to enrich the knowledge we already possess: 'in mobilizing what we already know and what we already feel, the narrative artwork can become an occasion for us to deepen our understanding of what we already know and feel' (Carroll, in Levinson 1998: 142). And Richard Eldridge has argued at length for art's capacity to present to us 'materials about which we do not know exactly how to feel and judge (Eldridge 2003a: 226). Artworks do not resolve this material—say a striking representation of a morally ambiguous practice—into a proposition that tells us *what* to feel and think about it. The force of their presentation of this material resides in the very act of working through it, for in so doing artworks bring to light the 'complex texture of our human lives' (Eldridge 2003a: 230).

[20] For helpful discussions of Cavell's concept of acknowledgement, see Mulhall (1994); Lamarque (1996); Eldridge (1997, 2003b); and Hammer (2002).

I will begin with a suggestive passage from *Must We Mean What We Say*:

It is not enough that I *know* (am certain) that you suffer, I must do or reveal something (whatever can be done). In a word, I must *acknowledge* it, otherwise *I do not know* what (yours, his) 'being in pain' means... The claim of sympathy may go unanswered. We may feel lots of things—sympathy, *Schadenfreude*, nothing. If one says that this is a failure to acknowledge another's suffering, surely this would not mean that we fail, in such cases, to *know* that he is suffering? It may or it may not.[21]

On a shallow reading it may appear that all that is being described here is an appropriate expression of a piece of possessed knowledge, say my reacting, as mere response behaviour, to my knowledge that you are suffering. But this is to miss the deeper cognitive point at play here—namely, that there is a form of understanding that is left unmentioned by our standard talk of knowledge, one that is revealed in our various successes and failures of acknowledgement.

The cases that best bring this form of understanding into view are those in which we find a failure of acknowledgement with an apparent success of knowledge. In the above passage, it is implied by my ability to describe you correctly as suffering that I possess knowledge of 'what suffering is'. I show by my accomplishment of identification that I know what counts as an instance of suffering. I reveal that I am competent enough with this concept to cut up reality according to it; and, if I can individuate objects according to a concept, I have met the minimum requirement for counting as a knower of this concept.

But a tension arises in certain cases, one that points up a limitation of the concept of knowledge for yielding a fully circumscribed notion of understanding. My failure of acknowledgement when I know that you are suffering tempts us to say that in some sense I cannot *really* know what suffering means. For, surely if I did, your suffering would make some claim on me, would spur some response

[21] Cavell (1969: 108).

to your condition, however minimal and of whatever sort. We find that our intuitions are jarred in these cases, for, as much as my act of identification tells us that I am a knower, my expression of this knowledge suggests that something must be amiss in my mind, that against everything I cannot *really* know this. Our intuitions are pulled in two directions: we want to say that what I do warrants as much as it argues against the idea that I really know what I am saying. So we have to ask what it is that is missing, for we know that something is. My knowledge is in place. But the failure of my knowledge to go on to take the form of acknowledgement reveals a hollowness in how I understand what it is that I know, an emptiness or confusion in some larger region of understanding that surrounds this knowledge.[22] Thus the questions become: How might we describe this region? What sort of understanding does it address?

To help answer these, imagine a person I will call the Simpleton. The Simpleton, we will agree, is a sort of *mere* knower. He looks at a wounded person—imagine that it is you—and rightly says 'you are in pain'. But the Simpleton expresses his knowledge in such a way that we find a certain vacancy in his grasp of what it is that he is saying. I ask him whether he thinks your injury is serious, to which he offers an earnest 'yes'. But he offers his 'yes' with no inflection of interest, without any gesture that hints that by this 'yes' he understands what *he* is thereby called on to do (say, as Cavell does, 'whatever can be done'). As I begin tending to you, I tell the Simpleton that he ought to call for an ambulance. He nods in sincere agreement and then falls still. And when I tell the Simpleton that you might not recover without his assistance, he responds with an honest 'that's right' and then lapses back into inactivity.

---

[22] What I am describing as a failure of acknowledgement may appear to have much in common with a traditional account of the problem of the freedom of the will, more specifically the problem of epistemic (or intellectual) akrasia. If one takes what I am describing as the failure of acknowledgement to be a species of epistemic akrasia, I would have no objections: perhaps at some level they are simply different ways of describing the same (or very similar) phenomenon. I thank Peter Goldie for pointing out this possibility to me.

Note that the Simpleton succeeds in every case of knowledge, for he consistently reveals that he knows the truth of the matter (that you are suffering, that this implies that you require aid, that the consequences will be severe should we ignore this...). But there is nothing more in the Simpleton's mind than this mere knowledge. The failure of acknowledgement we see in the Simpleton shows that he is capable only of the 'identification *of* pain, not *with* it'.[23] He has no further relation to your pain beyond his knowing it, beyond his ability correctly to identify your suffering and the nest of propositions this entails.[24] In this sense his knowledge is idle, lifeless, for his mind goes dead precisely when it ought to become animated. In a word, he is an idiot who just happens to know as much as we do, an eerie sort of *idiot savant*. The cognitive flaw lies not in his 'knowledge' but in his mind's inability to move from knowing to what this knowledge calls on one to do. What we see in the Simpleton is a failure to grasp what we might call the *demands* of knowledge, the claims knowledge makes *on us*. The hollowness we see in the Simpleton's mind is not an absence of proper knowledge but an incognizance, as it were, of the sets of responses to which this knowledge is tied and through which we naturally expect it to declare itself.

Let us look at a different failure of acknowledgement, that of a character we might call the Sadist. Both we and the Sadist succeed in identifying Medea as suffering. But precisely those aspects of the play that are tragic make it comic to the Sadist: Medea's suffering prompts the Sadist's laughter. His laugh is neither the laugh of the cynic who wants to mock the play's attempt to tug at our hearts nor of the crank who wants to be scandalous, should we think that he is just trying to disturb the pleasure we take in the play. It is a *sincere* belly laugh, without any tinge of callousness or posturing,

---

[23] This is a formulation Cavell is well known for exploiting. As he says in one of his various discussions of acknowledgement in *The Claim of Reason*: 'my identification of you as a human being is not an identification of you but *with* you' (Cavell 1979: 421).

[24] Lamarque (1996) finds in current neuropsychology an interesting parallel with failures of acknowledgement: the cognitive disorder found in those suffering from Capgra's Syndrome.

and shocking for this reason. He reacts to Jason's betrayal of Medea as though he is watching a burlesque. He bursts at Medea's murder of her children as though it is a punchline to an outrageously funny joke.

Naturally we are disturbed, for the Sadist strikes us as entirely deranged. Yet, just as with the Simpleton, we find that with every question we put to him the Sadist betrays that he knows what suffering is. Thus the derangement we detect in him is not a matter of his failure to perceive the world correctly, as though he sees something that is not really there. He sees precisely what is there—suffering—and he looks the lunatic because in his mind laughter issues from this knowledge.

We seem to see in the Sadist's response our concept of suffering grounded in a context alien to the one in which we commonly place it, the comic instead of the tragic. Horror films, whatever we may think of them as artworks, offer endless examples of this. What is disturbing in a film like Fritz Lang's *M* or a movie like Jonathan Demme's *Silence of the Lambs* is not merely Franz Becker's killing or Hannibal Lecter's cannibalism. The sense of the horrible these characters conjure in us is in large part a matter of their showing us how deformed and unsettling our concepts become when they are severed from the practices to which they are conventionally bound and wed with monstrous ones, 'love' as expressed through the act of murdering children, 'food' as the consumption of human flesh. Likewise, the Sadist's situating of 'suffering' in the laughable does not reveal an absence of knowledge so much as a displacement of it, a failure to station his knowledge of suffering in the web of contexts that is its natural home (the tragic, the pitiable, the sorrowful, whatever one wants). He seems so separate from us because the concepts we share with him make such a foreign claim on his mind. By his failure to hang his knowledge on the appropriate hook of response, the Sadist reveals a disfigurement of understanding, one consisting not of botched knowledge but rather of a broken link between his concepts and the regions of human experience and activity to which they are tied.

Now there are many things wrong with these two characters. Most are of the standard moral variety. They are probably in possession of rather vicious characters; they seem not to care much for what one should care for greatly, and much else besides. But, while these examples raise moral issues, my interest here is not in their moral dimension, narrowly conceived. Rather, I am especially interested in how the moral failures here suggest certain *cognitive* failures. They are failures of moral understanding, certainly. But it is the issue of understanding itself that I wish to explore.

What the Simpleton and Sadist bring to view very clearly is a certain flaw of mind, one that is revealed by their failures to acknowledge (*at all*, in the case of the Simpleton; *aright*, in the case of the Sadist) the knowledge they share with us. The Simpleton suffers a failure to understand how knowledge, we might say, ought to configure the knower as an actor on the stage of life. Earlier I called this a failure to grasp the 'claims knowledge makes *on us*', and the Sadist shows us that these 'claims' are akin to what is often described as *claims to a community*, that through our successes and failures of acknowledgement we announce our participation in (or estrangement from) a shared 'form of life', as Wittgenstein would put it. It is a form of understanding that concerns not a grasp of the 'truth of the matter', knowledge of the nature of the bit of reality before them. It consists in a mind's awareness of what is better described as the *role* a piece of knowledge plays in a form of life.

A further point these odd characters help us to see is that genuine understanding is never value neutral, is never *merely* conceptual, at least not when it concerns human reality. To count as possessing full understanding of something, we must reveal not only that we have the relevant concepts and representational capacities. We must also show that we are *alive* to those patterns of value, significance, and meaning that are given expression in the aspects of the world we otherwise merely know. We do this not by revealing that we are in possession of the right propositions or descriptions, say by asserting, correctly, 'an ambulance is needed' or 'this person is in pain'. In fact, when we attempt to elaborate this sort of understanding, to bring into full view just what it is, we tend to do so by depicting not what one says but what one *does* when one knows something. We offer examples of how someone *invests* herself in the particular scene she knows (or refuses to, say in a character such as Bartleby), of how a piece of knowledge should function to turn the knower into a certain sort of *agent*. We describe a type of response, a kind of gesture, that embodies this understanding. That is, we give an account of how one acknowledges what one knows.

Note that an act of acknowledgement, like a moral response, is a kind of *dramatic* gesture, and that the understanding it embodies itself has a certain dramatic structure. An act of acknowledgement is a way of giving life to what it is that we know, of bringing it into the public world, not unlike the way in which an actor gives life to a character, or an artist makes manifest an inner emotion through a perfectly rendered expression. Understanding, if fully possessed, establishes a type of dramatic relation between a knower and the world. It places us in the world as agents who are responsive to the range of values and experiences that are the mark of human reality. Recall that the term 'drama' itself comes to us from the Greek for 'action' or 'deed' (*drama*; adj. *dramatikos*), and that 'dramatic' has in its more contemporary usage the sense of doing something with an emotional investment or charge.[25] These are, in effect, the signs of the form of understanding brought to view by the notion of acknowledgement.

I will conclude this section by bringing the concept of acknowledgement in line with an aspect of the language–reality relation that we have already discussed—namely, the role criteria have in securing our alignment with the world. The Simpleton and the Sadist offer us an occasion to refine the concept of criteria introduced in the previous chapter, and I introduced these characters in part to lead us back to this notion.

---

[25] I am indebted to Richard Shusterman (2001) for his discussion of the concept of the dramatic.

Criteria, as earlier discussed, have the role of explaining how language presents an orientation towards reality.[26] In a word, criteria specify what *counts* as reality for us. As Stanley Cavell and Stephen Mulhall have noted, in explaining this we can identify two allied yet discrete ways in which criteria tell us 'what counts'.[27] What I want to add to this is that these two senses of 'counting' in turn illustrate how the concepts of knowledge and acknowledgement each express a distinct cognitive purchase on the world.

My discussion of criteria up to this point has dwelt largely on the first sense of how criteria tell us 'what counts,' as a matter of what counts as an instance of a concept—one thing a stone, another a sufferer, this a rose, that a jealous husband. This sense of 'counts' concerns how language, through criteria, specifies 'what kind of object anything is', as an issue of the individuation and identity of the nature of the things in the world around us. Yet in the previous chapter we also saw how deeply cultural the notion of criteria is. We saw that in specifying our criterial relation to reality we are not led to metaphysical or theoretical objects but are rather brought into contact with the fabric of our social practices, of those patterns of mutual agreement that account for how we achieve a shared sense of our world.

To borrow an ugly term from ethics, for a moment at least, the second sense in which understanding is linked to a notion of how a criterion counts is *axiological*, broadly put. If the first sense

---

[26] Cavell (1979: 316).

[27] I am especially indebted to Stephen Mulhall's discussion of this. As he puts it: 'We might summarize the role of criteria by saying that criteria tell us what *counts* as an instance of something. But this link between the concept of criteria and the concept of counting involves two facets of the meaning of the latter term... On the one hand, criteria are criteria of individuation: in determining what counts *as* a table, they determine whether any given object falls under that particular concept or rather some other... On the other hand, criteria manifest what counts *for* human beings: by determining how human beings count one thing from another, how they conceptualize the world, criteria trace the distinctions and connections which matter to them—the distinctions which count. The structure of the concepts themselves is an expression of human interests, of which aspects of the world we deem significant enough to wish to get a grip on' (Mulhall 1994: 153).

emphasizes our ability to speak of things in the world—a matter of what counts as an instance of ϕ—the second sense emphasizes the place of these things in our world—a matter of why and how ϕ counts for us, how and why it *matters*. As the first sense in which a criterion counts emphasizes our ability to represent the world correctly, the second sense highlights the capacity to see the consequence of those aspects of the human world so represented. This sort of understanding designates an awareness of what is *at stake* when we represent the world in certain ways; it reveals a grasp of how an object or event should function to *engage* us with the world when we describe it as thus and such. To this extent, it is a distinctly cultural form of understanding, for it has as its target not merely objects and their identity conditions but the values, cares, and concerns that define the character of our particularly human practices and experiences. The notion of criteria unites under one concept these affiliated yet distinct aspects of our cognitive purchase on reality, the conditions of worldly identification, and the cultural values that are expressed in these very conditions.

When we speak of knowledge, we describe a certain intellectual relation to the world. And what the Simpleton and the Sadist showed us is that this leaves unmentioned its 'flesh', its concreteness. The concept of criteria underscores this point, that we have both an intellectual and an embodied relation to the world. Likewise, the movement from knowing to acknowledging reveals a mind that is in full possession of its criteria, that it grasps how they 'count' in this dual sense, and thus grasps them fully. If the notion of criteria unites into one concept the (broadly put) semantic and social dimensions of language's alignment with the world, the concept of acknowledgement repeats this union at the level of a mind's awareness of the world.

This discussion of criteria should also make clear that the concept of acknowledgement does not specify a region of mind that is *different* from that which knowledge concerns, if we mean by this that acknowledgement describes some alternative or independent

Beyond Truth and Triviality

route to worldly understanding.[28] Just as when we discuss the two ways in which a criterion 'counts' we are not speaking of two distinct criteria, when we move from knowledge to acknowledgement we are not crossing borders between foreign spheres of understanding. The difference is between a completeness and an incompleteness of understanding, not between two disparate ways of relating to the world. Knowledge, as I said at the beginning of this discussion, must go on to take the form of acknowledgement—otherwise there is a sense in which we cannot *really* know what it is that we are saying. And what is meant by this is that these two concepts describe a *completeness* of understanding, as two elements that together assert an achievement of one motion of mind. In a word, acknowledgement describes knowledge as *fulfilled*. The concepts of knowledge and acknowledgement are confederate notions. Together they function to record this completeness of understanding.

If what I have said in this section is reasonable, then surely we want to describe the difference between the acknowledger and the Simpleton, the sane person and the Sadist, as cognitive. In each case, though the same knowledge is in place, we see drastically different manifestations of intelligence, clear differences in the understanding of the meaning of the words one is using. If we are tempted to refuse to call the feature of understanding announced by the concept of acknowledgement 'cognitive', I would venture that it is because—oddly and sadly—we do not have the right cognitive term to describe it, though my argument is that 'acknowledgement' will work quite well for this purpose. To give into this temptation is to allow the vocabulary of truth and knowledge to hoard all our cognitive terms, to treat them as the sole terms of cognitive illumination. And this betrays a rather severe philosophical prudishness, a refusal to

[28] As Cavell puts it: 'Acknowledging is not an alternative to knowing but an interpretation of it. Incorporating, or inflecting, the concept of knowledge, the concept of acknowledgment is meant, in my use, to declare that what there is to be known philosophically remains unknown not through ignorance (for we cannot just not know what there is to be known philosophically, for example that there is a world and I and others in it) but through a refusal of knowledge, a denial, or a repression of knowledge, say even a killing of it' (Cavell 1988: 51).

call 'cognitive' a concept that expresses the fulfilment of knowledge just because it cannot be described in the precise vocabulary of knowledge. If acknowledgement reveals a significant dimension of understanding, if it describes a completeness of our grasp of our world, I see no reason at all not to call it cognitive.

3.3. LITERATURE AND THE FULFILMENT OF KNOWLEDGE

We can now return to the anti-cognitivist sceptic. Our problem was this: the sceptic challenged that, even if it is the case that literature presents reality to view, it in no way yields knowledge of it in this act of presentation; hence his claim that literature does nothing more than offer idle visions of a world we already well know. This much, he argued, flows from the source of our trouble in this chapter, the problem of cognitive familiarity. But what we are beginning to see is that the charge of triviality does not so easily follow from the fact of familiarity, and this is the point on which the sceptic's case hangs. If 'knowing' does not exhaust the range of possible cognitive experience, then a textual form that cannot lead us to knowledge of the world will not on this count alone be cognitively trivial.

In fact, we can accept that we know those corners of the world literature brings to view (or, again, at least that it cannot be the case that we come to know them through literature). We can accept this because it turns out to be a claim the humanist can graciously embrace, for it gives him a ground on which to proceed. It is not a problem set in his way but a point of departure. There is a form of cognition that itself presupposes the possession of knowledge to take shape. And the humanist can argue that literature, by standing upon our knowledge of the world, is thereby able to address this further region of understanding.

The requirement of knowledge (or the impossibility of acquiring knowledge through literature), far from stifling the possibility of a theory of the cognitive value of literature, turns out to be a remarkably meagre condition. It requires only that we are as smart as the Simpleton, as aware of the world as the Sadist, which is not much of a requirement at all. What the humanist wants to say is that literature can operate on the form of worldly understanding that these characters make visible to us. Now most of us are not as lacking of mind as these characters, and I do not want to be misread as making the ridiculous claim that literature assumes that we are all of us simpletons and functions to fill in what would remain an empty region of mind without it.[29] But surely most of us, with our in varying degrees less dramatic lives, do not possess a comprehension of how jealousy or suffering configure human life with the precision of detail and depth of vision we find in the works of Shakespeare and Dostoevsky (as it is sometimes said, literature is a great 'force of particularization'). We might recall Iris Murdoch's elegant phrasing of what is really the same idea: 'The greatest art shows us the world... with a clarity which startles and delights us because we are not used to looking at the real world at all.'[30]

The point I want to make here is that the concept of acknowledgement presents to us a way of seeing how this 'startling' clarity of literature's presentation of life can reveal something important about our cognitive relation to the world.

---

[29] An earlier version of this chapter invited a misreading I am here attempting to prevent—namely, that if we try to solve the problem by claiming that literature can offer acknowledgement—the claim the humanist is obviously directing us towards—this implies that literature has cognitive value only for those of us as void of mind as the Simpleton (I thank Sonia Sedivy for bringing this misreading to my attention). My inclination is to say that this way of reading the humanist is about as right, and as wrong, as reading the claim that philosophy's cognitive value consists in its offering knowledge as implying the claim that it therefore takes as its audience the idiots among us, that it has value for those of us with *no* knowledge—as though the claim that Plato can illuminate the good life suggests that one who stands to learn from him must be in utter darkness about all matters moral and ethical. The problem, as I understand it to be a problem, is not whether literature can correct ignorance or fill in utterly blank spaces in our worldly understanding but most basically one of whether literature can *declare, expose, map* a certain territory of our cognitive relation to reality. Of course, if we can show the latter, we can then say that literature can work, when needed, to correct the former, and so we open the door to any number of forms of cognitive therapy literature might offer.

[30] Murdoch (1970: 34).

Now there is nothing surprising we need to reveal about literature to make explicit precisely how literature might do this. There is certainly no need to imitate the truth-seeking humanist and try to twist literary content in the hope of finding a way to treat it as a participant in the same game played by philosophy. We give up this idea altogether, and with it the temptation to commit literarily unconscionable acts such as treating Othello the Moor as a proposition about the way the world is who just masquerades as a fiction in Shakespeare's tragedy, literature in general as a form of truth-directed discourse that for some reason chooses to moonlight as fictional narrative. If we link literature to acknowledgement rather than to knowledge, we can see that explaining the cognitive value of literature requires none of this. We can accept, that is, that literature does the only thing it incontestably does: present fictional lives lived in a fictional world, fictions that, while bringing our world into view, nevertheless do not state truths about this world.

Simply put, the humanist wants us to see that if, for example, Othello is to illuminate our understanding of jealousy, we do not at all need Othello to tell us anything about what jealousy is. To make the move from knowledge to acknowledgement, we need only Othello himself, this supreme animator of the knowledge of jealousy we bring to the text. We do not need to find a way to get Othello to forfeit his fictionality and become something he manifestly is not (say a truth claim presented as a dramatic persona) to secure a connection with the cognitive. We need precisely his fictionality, this Moor of Venice who offers us the story 'of one not easily jealous, but being wrought, perplex'd in the extreme' (v. ii. 345–7). It is in this, in this fictional tale, that we see all we need to see to understand how *Othello* can effect its particular enlightenment. Acknowledgement requires just what literature is in a position to give it: narrative, a story of human activity. Let me explain.

Harold Bloom has said that Desdemona 'is our word for Romantic love'.[31] Likewise, and with the same instructive bombast, let us say

---

[31] Bloom (1998: 73).

that Othello is our word for jealousy. Now if this is so, a fair summary of the sceptic's argument in this chapter is that we nevertheless do not, cannot, learn this word from literature. But what the humanist argues is that this is no loss, that Othello's gift to the mind lies not in his giving us knowledge of the word but in the ways in which he can embody this word, bring it to life, and give it shape, structure, and vitality. Othello is only a fiction. But a fiction, as I argued in the last chapter, is nonetheless capable of bringing our world to view. And what we are beginning to see is that, in bringing it into view, *Othello* does not merely reflect our world back to us in the same form in which it presupposes that we are familiar with it. *Othello* returns to us this knowledge as placed on the stage of cultural practice and human comportment. In this sense, the drama in which Othello finds himself gives the understanding we bring to this artwork a dramatic structure. Cultural understanding is in essence the grasp of the various dramas that constitute human experience, and so a textual form such as literature that speaks to understanding *dramatically* does all that is needed to carry out an important cognitive service.

As we saw, the concept of knowledge is silent about whether our understanding of the world is vital or idle; we saw that, when our knowledge has not gone on to take the form of acknowledgement, we have minds that know but whose knowledge is oddly immaterial, strangely removed from the world, as though we see it from a distance. Of course, this distance comes in degrees, ranging from the extreme case of a character such as the Simpleton to what I presume is the state of most of us—namely, reasonably acculturated people but nevertheless people who have not been afforded the wealth of experience and insight that would come with having lived the lives chronicled in our greatest works of literary narrative. Literature takes this as its cue, speaking to the mind by addressing and attempting to overcome this distance. Literature has a unique and profound ability to present our world to us not as a conceptual object but as a living world. And it is thereby able to take what is dull, wooden, or tenuous in our understanding of how our words and our concept unite us with our world and inject it with this vitality of understanding.[32]

What literary narratives are able to do especially well is take the concepts we bring to our reading of a work and present them back to us as concrete forms of human engagement. When we read *Othello*, *Notes from Underground* or *Bartleby the Scrivener*, we see jealousy, suffering, and alienation presented not as mere 'ideas' but as very precisely shaped human situations. And this contextualization of these concepts, this act of presenting them to us in concrete form, is literature's contribution to understanding, the particular light it has to shine on our world. Literary works do not offer conceptual knowledge, if by this we mean that they offer an elaboration of the nature of some aspect of our world, delivered, as it were, in a propositional package. Nor need they if they are to have a claim to cognitive value. If they embody a form of understanding, it will consist in a more literal act of embodiment—namely, in the capacity of a literary narrative to give substance to the range of values, concerns, and experiences that define human reality.

The vision of life we find in literary narratives shows us human practice and circumstance not from an abstracted, external perspective but from the 'inside' of life, in its full dramatic form. And, if the argument I gave in the last section is convincing, we can now see how this dramatic presentation of life might be an important cognitive achievement. This achievement does not consist in the stating of truths or the offering of knowledge of matters of fact. It is rather a matter of literature's ability to open up for us a world of value and significance and of all that this implies about our capacity to understand fully the import of various forms of human activity. Literary works' mode of engaging with the world is never narrowly or purely cognitive. Literature would not be *dramatic* if it were. But

---

[32] Peter de Bolla (2001) offers a very different, but fascinating, application of the concept of acknowledgement to art—specifically the poetry of Wordsworth—in *Art Matters* (2001). I unfortunately came upon this book too late to make use of it here.

it is precisely this drama we need if we are to have a textual form that is capable of documenting our particular way in the world.

When literary works are successful dramatic achievements, it is usually in part because they fashion a sense of what is at stake in the specific regions of human circumstance they bring to view. In this respect there is an interesting parallel between literary narratives and moral responses. Just as a moral response does not so much convey knowledge of an event as it gives expression to an agent's awareness of its significance, literary works, rather than stating truths about our world, bring to light the consequence, the import, of those aspects of reality they bring before us. It is in this respect that literary works represent ways of acknowledging the world rather than knowing it.[33] A literary narrative is in effect a sustained dramatic gesture, a way not only of presenting some content or material but of responding to it.

Literature treats the world not as an object of knowledge but as a subject of human concern. And this itself is a cognitive accomplishment, a way of bearing witness to the world. This gives us reason to speak of literature as engaged in a form of worldly investigation, of a sort that is markedly different from what we find in standard works of enquiry. It is a dramatic investigation. But human life itself is dramatic in nature, and so literary works, in their characteristically literary form, would appear to be perfectly built for its exploration. The category of the dramatic is, I take it, a proper *literary* category; the dramatic achievement of a literary work is intimately bound up with its aesthetic success and artistic accomplishment. Thus, contrary to a long-standing fear, to speak of the cognitive achievement of a literary work is not to speak of something altogether other than its properly aesthetic and literary features. Accordingly, we can respect

---

[33] I thank an anonymous referee for OUP and Espen Hammer for pointing out that an earlier draft of this chapter suggested that it is *readers* who do the acknowledging here, which would be an odd claim, since it is unclear what it would mean for a reader to acknowledge fictions (we cannot interact with them, for example). The argument I am offering is that it is the *literary work*, a *narrative*, that is engaged in the relevant act of acknowledgement and response, not readers.

the textual constraint when defending literary cognitivism. The form of insight literature trades in is bound up with the internal structure of a literary work. In fact, it is inseparable from it.[34] The insight into life we find in a great novel is the novel itself, as the New Critics liked to remind us. It is woven into the fabric of the story and the specific ways in which it configures and gives dramatic expression to its subject matter.

Let me return briefly to the notion of criteria to give a more precise statement of how literature accomplishes this. If the humanist claimed in the previous chapter that literature's manner of worldly presentation is a matter of bringing to view our criteria for the way our world is, we saw here that literature does not offer knowledge of these criteria in this act of presentation. But, as we also saw, the sceptic requires that we know these criteria only in the incomplete way in which the Simpleton and the Sadist know them. He requires only a mere awareness of how they 'count' the world by offering us grounds for identifying and describing its furniture correctly. This is what is presupposed by our ability to identify Othello as jealous, Dostoevsky's confessor as a sufferer; this is what literature assumes we know, these basic grounds for identifying 'what sort of object anything is'. This leaves open for literature's exploration an immense region of worldly understanding, at any rate more than enough for the humanist to show that literature's exploration of this is an important form of cognitive labour.

The humanist's response to the sceptic's challenge amounts to the claim that literature, while assuming our knowledge of how criteria 'count' in the first sense, is able to go on to expose their other face, their cultural and axiological dimension; that literature is able to piece our criteria together, and, in so doing, piece together the two basic facets of the mind's relation to the world, the intellectual and the embodied, knowing and acknowledging. In short, literature can reveal our criteria in their *completeness*. In this respect, if literature

---

[34] See Katherine Thomson-Jones (2005) for an interesting recent discussion of the inseparability of the form of a literary work and its cognitive value.

cannot offer knowledge of the world, it is able to take our knowledge and return it to us as *fulfilled*.

We often think that the gap between mind and reality is closed by knowledge, that, when we come into possession of truths about the way the world is, we overstep the space between thought and reality. The concept of acknowledgement reveals the possibility of a residual gap; it shows that the concept of knowledge alone does not express understanding as it reaches all the way into the world. The claim the humanist wants to secure is that it is this remaining divide that literature is capable of addressing and overcoming. Thus it is not merely 'clarification'—to borrow an apt term from Noël Carroll—of our *beliefs* and *knowledge* that is going on here, as though all we gain from this a clearer sense of our knowledge.[35] We do get this, but we get something else in addition. The ways in which a literary work operates on our understanding is a matter of relating our beliefs, our concepts, our knowledge, to something *outside* them: our world and the forms of human activity and circumstance we find in it. It is this often elusive link between, as one might put it, the epistemic and the cultural that literature exposes and explores. This is as much revelation as it is clarification.

Take the following example, one that I hope will clarify the point I am urging. Imagine those texts we take to define our literary tradition laid out in a line. Next to it, we lay out those texts that define our philosophical tradition. Someone—imagine not a simpleton but someone more like an alien—puts to us the question of what each of these textual traditions documents about our relation to the world, what she, should she read through each of them, would come to learn about our world. Most of us would find at least half of this question easy to answer. We would say, whatever else we might say, that what those works that constitute our philosophical heritage attempt to trace and give testament to is our conceptual relation to reality, what our culture takes to be its reserve of philosophical knowledge.

[35] See Carroll, in Levinson (1998).

Now there is an initial difficulty when we turn to our literary heritage. We wonder what literature, given the uniqueness of its manner of worldly presentation (namely, *fictional* presentation), could possibly record about our relation to the world. What the humanist has shown is that the mistake is to think that we need to find a way to describe literature as in some way doing what philosophy does (a temptation many humanists have felt since Plato pitted poets against philosophers). And what is liberating about the humanist's argument is that we now see that we can avoid this temptation without fearing that we will thereby make literature speechless about our cognitive relation to our world.

Simply put, if those textual forms such as philosophy trace our culture's claims to knowledge, literature, far from being inferior, sets its goal further. By weaving the knowledge it assumes into the fabric of the social, literature traces and gives testament to the bond between our words, our concepts, and the concrete body of our culture. And, in doing so, literature records not the first but the final word in our culture's awareness of its world, the word that effectively concludes the story we have to offer of the nature of our world as we experience it and find ourselves within it. If we had only philosophy texts, we would have a chronicle of only half of our relation to our world. There would be a silence about what lies on the other side of this gap that knowledge alone does not quite bridge. Literature is that corner of intellectual activity that archives how understanding fully crosses this remaining divide between mind and world. It is not in competition with philosophy, but, in its highest form, literature is the completion of its project.

4
The Work of Criticism

I have, thus far, been defending humanism from the standpoint of the 'problem of fiction', that is, by attempting to show that we can see—and a sort of seeing that is cognitively significant—reality in texts that seem altogether content to speak about the imaginary and the unreal. This is, of course, how the problem is usually approached, since it is the fictionality of literary works that causes such trouble for the humanist. What is odd, however, is that recent literary aesthetics has had virtually nothing to say about this matter in an area of debate one would think just as natural a place to address it: the theory of interpretation.[1] After all, the theory of interpretation is concerned with issues of textual meaning and aboutness; and the question of whether literature can be revelatory of reality would seem at least partially to be a question of whether literary works can 'mean' something of cognitive consequence or be 'about' reality in any epistemologically interesting sense. Discussions of the cognitive value of literature and the nature of interpretation are two of the liveliest in current aesthetics, and it is striking that there has been no explicit attempt to build a bridge between the two. It is the prospect of fruitfully uniting these two areas of literary aesthetics that I explore in this chapter.

---

[1] The work of Eileen John can be read as an implicit exception to this claim. Her work is marked by an interest in showing that, of those works of fiction that put on offer a form of philosophical or conceptual knowledge, the moment of cognitive acquisition 'is apt to occur primarily in our responses to the work—such works call for the reader or audience to be philosophers' (John 1998: 331). I take it that locating the mechanism of cognitive acquisition in our *responses* to a work of fiction—rather than in some feature of the text itself—is tantamount to situating it in our interpretative activities.

What a discussion of interpretation shall help us address is a worry that has probably been lurking in the mind of the reader for the past two chapters, a nagging feeling that something cannot be quite right in all this. The worry is captured well by Peter Lamarque: 'The particulars presented in a novel are *fictional*, and how can any view, however objective, of *fictional* particulars, give us truth? Ex hypothesi, it is not a view of the real world.'[2]

Ignoring the question of truth, which I put to rest in the previous chapter, the question at hand is what it might mean to *read* literature as a humanist. That is, what could it possibly mean to claim, as I have, that we can regard content explicitly presented as fictional as also revelatory of reality? For, if we are witnessing fictions, to what extent can our attention also be drawn to reality? 'Ex hypothesi, it is not a view of the real world.' How can the stance we take towards fictional content be open to reality in the way the humanist requires it to be? What is needed, in short, is an account of what the thesis of literary humanism amounts to as a claim about how we are engaged by literary works, about how we *read* them.

The question that needs to be addressed is in essence a matter of how we might reconcile two stances. The first stance is what philosophers call 'the fictive stance', the basic stance we take towards the content of literary works.[3] The second might be called the 'worldly stance', the stance that describes our attitude when we appreciate some described state of affairs as (plainly put) functioning to illuminate reality. We might in turn say that each of these stances describes a frame within which we interpret various types of texts and discourses—namely, whether they are to be read as revealing something about our world or a fictional world.

The humanist, of course, wants to say that the frame of fiction can also offer a window to the world, that one and the same appreciative attitude can be directed towards both the fictional and the real. If someone is sympathetic to the theory of humanism I have offered

---

[2] Lamarque (1996: 105).
[3] The expression 'fictive stance' was introduced by Lamarque and Olsen (1994).

in the previous chapters, she will not believe that reality cannot be found in works of fiction. But the theoretical arguments of the previous chapters need to be brought down to earth and addressed on the level of how we respond to literary content. And, for this, the humanist needs a theory of interpretation.

4.1. INTERPRETING WORDS, INTERPRETING WORLDS

At first glance it is very hard to see how a theory of interpretation could be of much use to the humanist. I have argued throughout that literary works do not make claims about reality, indeed that they do not in any literal sense *speak* about the world. And, if we give up the attempt to ground humanism on a picture of literary works themselves as trying, simply put, *to tell* us something about the world, how will a theory of interpretation help us here? For, on a very common conception, interpretation concerns precisely this: the activity of bringing to light what a literary work is trying to say. Indeed, according to an entrenched view, literature is primarily a medium through which a writer conveys a meaning, makes a claim, urges a point, *says* something. Is not the issue for the interpreter simply to grasp the meaning a literary work is attempting to convey? And, if we part with this idea, as the approach I will urge claims that in a crucial respect we should, to what extent are we still talking about interpretation?

In one sense it is obvious that interpretation does concern what a literary work 'says' or attempts to 'convey' in a straightforward linguistic sense. For example, we often have to engage in disambiguation in the presence of semantic infelicities such as vague descriptions, unintelligible sentences, misused or misprinted words, and the like. Consider the oft-cited example of 'tender' accidentally becoming 'tinder' upon the printing of Hart Crane's poem 'Thy Nazarene and Tinder Eyes', or that, as one moves between the various folios and quartos, Hamlet's 'oh that this too too sullied flesh would melt' becomes 'solid flesh' and 'sallied flesh'. And surely much of what we must do when reading works such as James Joyce's *Finnegans Wake* or William Faulkner's *The Sound and the Fury* is attempt to give sense to the almost endless semantic convulsions of their language. Interpretation in these cases is a matter of settling the sense of the language of a text, of assigning a determinate meaning to some ambiguous or otherwise linguistically curious feature of it. This is an activity virtually all literary works call upon at one point or another, and I nowhere here want to deny this. Since this concerns the attempt to render clear the language of a literary work, I shall call this sort of meaning 'linguistic meaning' and the interpretative activity it is tied to 'linguistic interpretation'.[4]

But a problem arises when we realize that we are talking about something more interesting, and much more philosophically challenging, when we speak of meaning in literary-critical contexts, especially meaning of the variety humanists tend to elicit from literary works. When we ask about the 'meaning' of a literary work in a humanistic sense, we do not usually have in mind *word* or *sentence* meaning. We ask what the *text* means, what sense we can attribute to the literary object itself rather than to its constitutive sentences. In this case we are speaking of a variety of meaning that stands over and above the express meaning of the language of the text. Think of the habit of treating William Shakespeare's *The Tempest* as partly 'about' the survival, or destruction (depending on one's reading), of reason and culture when confronted with savagery, though what Shakespeare in fact wrote speaks instead of a certain Prospero, a stranded Milanese scholar and aristocrat, and Caliban, a monster he enslaves. Consider when we say of Herman Melville's *Bartleby the Scrivener* that Bartleby's refusals 'mean' something about estrangement as a condition of modern life, while all Bartleby ever actually says is 'I

---

[4] See Cooper (2003) for an account of linguistic meaning as well as an argument against the idea that meaning is exclusively linguistic in nature, to both of which I am indebted to here.

would prefer not'. Think of when we claim that Samuel Coleridge's *Kubla Khan* offers an insight into the nature of poetic inspiration, despite the fact that when we examine the language of this poem we just find talk of pleasure domes and seething chasms. For reasons that will become clearer below, I shall call this sort of meaning 'critical' and the activity it concerns 'critical interpretation'.[5] This is the sort of meaning and interpretative activity I am concerned with here (and which I shall ultimately enlist in my defence of humanism).

Now, since literary works are, as the saying goes, 'pieces of language', an interpreter is clearly talking about a linguistic object when articulating critical meanings of this variety. But they are an odd sort of meaning, for they are not descriptive of any feature of the language of these works, certainly not of anything these works in any literal sense say. There is a clear dependence of critical meaning on the language of a literary work, for the interpreter offers a critical interpretation as a way of understanding a literary work, and he or she would not, presumably, understand a work *this* way if its language were other than it is. However, the concept of interpretation is intimately linked to the concept of understanding—of making sense of something—and the problem here is that it is not quite the language of the text that the interpreter is trying to understand better. We can imagine, for example, a literary work so simply and clearly written (and probably dull for these reasons) that (i) it requires no linguistic interpretation and (ii) an interpreter finds it rich in critical meaning. So critical interpretation seems not to be a species of linguistic interpretation, for it is an activity that can be engaged when the latter is not. Thus what we want to know is: what exactly

---

[5] With 'critical meaning' I introduce a term of art, and I intend it to refer only to the sort of critical activity I describe here. I use it as a broad concept that is intended to range over many of the varieties of meaning that we attribute to literary works that cannot be identified with the linguistic meaning of the works. Also, it might strike one as more natural to call this thematic meaning, but I have opted against this. Thematic meaning (and, I imagine, many cases of symbolic and metaphorical meaning) can at times be an instance of critical meaning—it will depend on the example—but it is too narrow a concept to capture what I am after, though there are obvious similarities.

is this sort of meaning, what generates it, of what is it descriptive, if not the linguistic meaning of the literary work?

There may be a temptation here to go deeper into the philosophy of language in search of more refined senses of conveyed meaning with which to explain critical meaning. For example, one might be inclined to look towards a notion of implied or indirect meaning: meaning that is conveyed through, but that cannot be identified with, the express or 'surface' meaning of a piece of language. There are two frameworks in which I can imagine one trying to develop this line of thought, applying, with some adjustments, either (i) a version of intentionalism: the idea that literary meaning is to be identified with a conception of a real or postulated (hypothetical) author's intended meaning; or (ii) a version of conventionalism: the idea that literary meaning is determined by public linguistic conventions (as opposed to authorial intentions), broadly construed.[6] Conventionalism and intentionalism are standard positions in contemporary theories of interpretation—indeed, they are often treated as marking the two poles of possible positions one may assume in the debate—and each has its own way of being helpful. My doubt here concerns only their suitability for illuminating critical meaning. Let me offer a few words as to why.

A conventionalist in the theory of interpretation might argue something like the following. We know, for example, that the sentence 'you needn't come in tomorrow' conveys or, more accurately, implies the proposition 'you are fired' when uttered in certain contexts, even though this meaning cannot be tethered to the semantic value of the sentence in fact uttered. What typically happens in cases like this is that we have knowledge of relevant linguistic conventions (that have reference to the conditions under which an utterance is made), which in turn build a bridge between the express and implied meaning of the sentence uttered. Thus the philosopher

---

[6] For a clear and helpful overview of conventionalism and intentionalism in the theory of interpretation, see Stecker, in Gaut and Lopes (2001). For a critical discussion of intentionalism, see Nathan, in Kieran (2006).

who embraces a conventionalist theory of interpretation might claim that critical meaning functions in much the same way. Meaning of the critical variety is not part of the surface meaning of the language of the text. Rather, there are appropriate linguistic conventions in place such that the language of the literary work can indirectly convey them. In short, critical meanings are implied propositions.

Here is the problem. There is not, nor would one expect there to be, *any* linguistic convention that unites the language of *The Tempest* with a claim about the survival of culture, nor one that weds the descriptions of Xanadu found in *Kubla Khan* with a proposition about the nature of poetic creation. It is entirely plausible to think that specific sentence or utterance types can bear a conventional link to specific implied propositions, but it is quite impossible to see how an entire work of imaginative fiction, composed of thousands of sentences, could ever come to bear such a link. It would be an extraordinary accomplishment if a culture could develop such complex conventions, and one can only wonder how it would go about instructing readers in their application. Critical meanings are too *sui generis*, too occasional, to think they can be explained with reference to general linguistic conventions.

Of course, once a critical tradition arises around a certain literary work, that work can come to bear a conventional link to a certain critical meaning, say as marking a culturally entrenched way of interpreting it (for instance, the habit, common since the mid-twentieth century, though not before it, of reading *Othello* as in part a meditation on race). But the question we are pursuing is what gets this process afoot in the first instance? What are critics identifying when they claim to have discovered a certain critical meaning in a literary work? It cannot be convention all the way down, for it is very unlikely that there are linguistic conventions at critics' disposal to guide them at this initial stage of critical discovery. And this is the stage we want to understand: what are critics describing when they claim to have uncovered a certain critical meaning, if not something the text actually says?

Intentionalism is a bit trickier.[7] I would think that some version of intentionalism is true of what I am calling linguistic interpretation. To give but one example, a conception of Shakespeare's intentions (or the intentions a competent audience would attribute to him, and so forth) might be required to settle whether Hamlet's flesh should be read as 'sullied' or 'sallied'.[8] I would also think that considerations of an actual or postulated author's intentions may at times offer a constraint on the range of critical meanings we can attribute to a work, and this in turn can help us understand what to do when we find ourselves confronted with conflicting critical interpretations (simply put, we disqualify those that cannot reasonably be attributed to a conception of what the author may have meant by his work). But note that this tells us nothing about how critical meanings themselves are generated—about what prods the interpreter to offer them up—and this is our question. It rather helps us understand what we should do with critical meanings once generated and found to be in conflict. Thus it sheds no light on what occasions the activity of critical interpretation itself, on just what the interpreter has identified when he or she attributes a critical meaning to a text.

Should intentionalists wish to make a stronger claim and argue that it is a consideration of authorial intentions that occasions critical interpretation (rather than merely acting as a constraint on those we already find ourselves inclined to attribute to an artwork), they court nonsense and literary barbarism. For it is the text that occasions critical interpretation, and to fall afoul of this fact is, as Monroe Beardsley would have it, to forget that the object of interpretative scrutiny is an artwork and not something beyond it.[9] Accordingly, it will be of no use to argue that critical meaning, though not manifest

---

[7] For an exhaustive and engaging account of intentionalism in the arts (and beyond), see Livingston (2005).

[8] For a popular account of a version of hypothetical intentionalism that gives a central role to the notion of an *audience* in imputing intentions that are in turn determinative of literary meaning, see Levinson, in Iseminger (1992), and in Krausz (2002).

[9] See Beardsley, in Iseminger (1992).

in the language of the text, forges its initial link to the text by way of a conception of an authorial intention that the text be read a certain way—a species of indirect meaning in this sense—for we have no way of explaining how this conception might be made present to interpreters such that it could call their critical activity into service. Presumably an interpreter does not offer the critical meaning in the example of *The Tempest* because he has some *independent* notion that Shakespeare might have meant this with his work, quite apart from anything he actually encounters in Shakespeare's creation. It *must* be something in the work; otherwise it would not occur to the interpreter to state it.[10] Now it may be, as so-called neo-Wittgensteinians like to point out, that authorial intentions are embedded in the language of the text, and thus that to describe the text will at times be by default to describe these intentions.[11] But, as we have seen, it does not seem to be the language of the text we are describing when engaged in critical interpretation, and so considerations of its language will hardly seem apt for helping us understand what prompts critical interpretation. Thus the questions still stand: what occasions critical meaning, what does it describe, what is its object?

There may still be an urge to continue mining the philosophy of language in search of ever more refined senses of linguistic meaning, more complex intentionalist or conventionalist models of indirect communication. One might expect such moves, given the extent to which so much aesthetics tends to concentrate on the linguistic dimension of interpretation. What I want to suggest, however, is that we do not need more linguistic categories and distinctions to understand this. We need more properly aesthetic ones. That is, we need to explore how literary works engage the imagination, and, in

[10] Against this one might protest that there are cases when the interpreter comes upon a comment in (say) an author's autobiographical notes that suggests to him a way of critically interpreting a text. This is true, but these cases are relatively rare. For this reason, it would be simply silly to claim that an interpretative activity as central as critical interpretation is *always* occasioned by some such discovery regarding an author's intentions, as though for every plausible critical interpretation we come upon we think that there must be implicit reference to a discovery of this sort.

[11] For the classic statement of this, see Lyas, in Iseminger (1992).

so doing, help bring about a unique object of appreciation, an object to which we simply have no access if we take a purely linguistic stance towards a literary work.

What I have in mind is the following. It is true that, when we look within a literary work we find only, as Bernard Harrison puts it, 'a tissue of words', but this tissue of words does something rather extraordinary when placed in the context of a literary work: it holds in place the texture of a *world*.[12] It is not an actual world, needless to say. It is rather what we commonly refer to as a fictional world. That literary works project fictional worlds is hardly news, of course. What is astonishing is that this feature of the literary work of art is virtually never mentioned in current work on interpretation. This, as one might put it, *world-generating* capacity of literary language is not shared in common with language in standard linguistic contexts. A hallmark of ordinary speech is the use of language to describe the world; a hallmark of literature is the use of language to create one. One would expect this difference between language in literary and standard communicative contexts to have important consequences for a theory of literary interpretation.[13]

There are many well-known ways of accounting for this world-generating capacity of literary language, almost all of which link it to a certain imaginative activity, as I discussed in previous chapters. Most theories of fiction tend to begin their account of our engagement with literature by emphasizing not primarily or especially the *meaning* the language of a text tries to convey but the *imaginings* it prescribes. Though the two are inseparable (an imagining is prescribed by the language of a text—that is, by its meaning in a straightforward linguistic sense) this switch in emphasis is important, for it reveals the uniqueness of our way of encountering language in literary

---

[12] Harrison, in Gibson and Huemer (2004: 93).

[13] I offer as evidence of this claim that in two of the most prominent anthologies on interpretation in analytical aesthetics—Iseminger (1992) and Krausz (2002)—none of the contributors concerns him or herself with the fictionality (what I call the world-generating capacity) of literary works and the implications this has for our interpretative encounters with them, with one exception. The exception is Goldman, in Krausz (2002), whose influence on my thinking here I would like acknowledge.

contexts. Literature disengages language from its standard function of referring to and representing the real world and instead places it in a certain imaginative space. This act is *transformative*: without it the language of a literary work is idle, non-referential, a representation of literally nothing at all. Representations require objects, for without them there is nothing to be represented. Literary works generate these objects and the fictional worlds they inhabit in tandem with the reader, by presenting their language as in effect a recipe for the imagination. It is through this that a text that would otherwise remain a continuous string of empty representations is given substance: that it is united with something for it to be about, to speak of, to describe.

This imaginative act, which opens up to view the fictional world of a work, makes possible a form of literary experience and appreciation to which we have no access if we take a purely linguistic stance towards a literary work. We might recall Bertrand Russell's infamous claim that statements descriptive of Hamlet are 'all false because there was no such man', which is an excellent example of the poverty of talk about literature when carried from a purely semantic perspective.[14] Literature's invocation of the imagination puts us into contact with something over and above, as it were, *Sinn*, the linguistic. It gives us a world, and to this extent a unique object of appreciative and interpretative scrutiny. If this is so, it suggests that this imaginative activity brings with it a distinct region of appreciation and interpretative investigation, in the form of the world a literary work brings to view. This is a region that is made available to appreciation only when we add to whatever linguistic stance we take towards a literary work this imaginative one. This is, to borrow a phrase from Peter Kivy, part of the 'performance of reading', the *activity* the reader engages when giving life to the world a literary work offers to appreciation.[15]

---

[14] Russell (1962: 275).
[15] See Kivy (2006), which contains the best discussion of which I am aware of the experience of reading literature. Unfortunately, this work was published just after I had completed the final draft of this book and so I was unable to make use of it.

We can now begin to say something positive about the nature of critical interpretation. It concerns, especially, the investigation of a world. The first thing to see is that worlds and what we find in them—characters, relationships, actions, events, among other things—have a sort of meaning and aboutness, but of a markedly different sort from words and sentences. The institutional oppression of a minority is *about* racism; the fact of love might *mean* that at the end of the day we are nevertheless capable of decent relationships. Or who knows? The point is that, to explain meaning and aboutness in these cases, we do not try to identify a linguistic entity such as a proposition or statement that is given expression in these features of our world. Worlds, unlike words, do not bear meaning in this way, nor need they to be meaningful. This is because, when applied to the structure of a world, of a practice, meaning and aboutness are in common usage tied to a notion not of signification but significance, not meaning in a linguistic sense but import in an explanatory sense.

This is what critical meaning is, meaning of the sort the literary humanist wishes to ascribe to literary works. Rather than directed at the recovery of linguistic meaning, critical interpretation marks a process of articulating patterns of salience, value, and significance in the worlds literary works bring to view. That is, critical interpretation marks the moment of our engagement with the world of the work, and it has as its goal the attempt to bring to light what we find of consequence in this world. If this is so, we can admit, for example, that *Bartleby the Scrivener* literally says nothing about modern alienation. But, for all that, it is not quite silent on the matter. It speaks about it not because it offers a word to this effect; as a form of literary communication, it is because it offers a world to this effect. And it is part of the critic's task to devise an interpretative framework that can render explicit the meaning, the significance, of human life as configured in the world Melville created for us.

Let me offer two examples of critical interpretation to help give shape to my point. Consider Terry Eagleton, who finds in Virginia Woolf's *To the Lighthouse* a vision of a common human struggle:

The point for Lily is to distance herself from the image of Mrs Ramsey to the point where she can freely acknowledge its influence. Her art allows her to do both, drawing the image of Mrs Ramsey closer yet 'placing' her, and so in a way triumphing over her. This illustrates a more general truth. Only by acknowledging the sources of our being, acknowledging our unsavoury historical heritage, can we have the power to free ourselves from them. If we are to sever ourselves from the maternal body and move beyond it, it can only be by recognizing our own continuing dependence on it.[16]

Cleanth Brooks, in his classic interpretation of Faulkner's *The Sound and the Fury*, begins by claiming that the work offers a 'progression from murkiness to increasing enlightenment' as it 'dramatizes for us with compelling urgency a situation we have come to accept almost as our own'. This urgency, he argues, resides in its presentation of a certain picture of modern circumstance:

The decay of the Compsons can be viewed, however, not merely with reference to the Southern past but to the contemporary scene. It is tempting to read it as a parable of the disintegration of modern man. Individuals no longer sustained by familial and cultural unity are alienated and lost in private worlds. One thinks here not merely of Caddy, homeless, the sexual adventuress adrift in the world, or of Quentin, out of touch with reality and moving inevitably to his death, but also and even primarily of Jason, for whom the break-up means the active rejection of claims and responsibilities, and with it, a sense of liberation.[17]

The critical activity in Eagleton's case is a matter of placing Lily's relation to her painting and its subject in a broader context of human activity—namely, the struggle to overcome what we find ugly and shameful in ourselves without denying who we in fact are. According to Eagleton, the text is in part *about* this struggle. In Brooks's example, the Compson family holds in place a picture of the world in which the pursuit of the personal leads necessarily to estrangement from others, even as, one might add, a retreat to the public (family, community) is rather bleakly revealed to be just a more complex

---

[16] Eagleton (2005: 326).
[17] All references to Brooks are in Faulkner (1994: 292).

form of isolation. This is part of what Brooks takes the text *to mean*. That is, each work is read as registering—though differently and perhaps incompatibly—certain visions of our relation to ourselves and to others, and thus of something about our way in the world.

Note that we will find none of this given mention in *To the Lighthouse* or *The Sound and the Fury*. Indeed, if literary interpretation is thought to be tied only to an attempt to render clear the meaning of text, and if this, in turn, is conceived as a largely linguistic enterprise, critical interpretations of this sort are bound to seem gratuitous, perhaps senseless, for these texts literally say nothing of the sort. Vindicating this sort of critical—ultimatitely humanistic—discourse requires situating it not in the search to render clear the linguistic act of a literary work but in the struggle to articulate the significance of its imaginative act. What critical passages such as Eagleton's and Brooks's bring to light is that the object of appreciation and interpretative scrutiny extends beyond the language that runs through the literary work of art. That is, they show us that, through our imaginative involvement with these works, we give ourselves access to a broader range of meaning and thus a richer appreciation of Woolf's and Faulkner's creations. What the critic's voice provides here is witness to this further region of literary meaning, to the capacity of literature to be about much more than what we find stated on the printed page.

Meaning of this sort is critical not only in the sense that it marks a prominent way literary critics speak in their interpretative activities. It is critical in the more interesting sense that it requires the voice of the interpreter—the critic's voice—to be made manifest. Critical interpretation is a matter of putting to words what we find of significance in the world of a work, of rendering discursively the import of what we witness imaginatively. However, this is still compatible with the notion of literary *communication*, that the reader is capturing (rather than simply fabricating) meaning when engaged in critical interpretation. Acknowledging this requires seeing that literary works offer meaning in a unique way, by using as the vehicle of communication a world rather than a string of words. Again, there is a clear dependence of the former on the latter, but the meanings we locate in the imaginative space created by a text cannot be reduced to meanings found in its linguistic space, and thus there is dependence without identity between these two sorts of meaning.

What would be dangerous to the idea of interpretation as a rational enterprise—that is, as an activity that is cognitively responsive to its object—would be a picture of critical interpretation that suggests that the critic *constructs* the world of a work in the very act of interpreting it. This is a consequence that often follows from theories of interpretation that give pride of place to the role of the reader in the generation of literary meaning (as we find in many deconstructive or neo-pragmatist accounts of interpretation). I hope that what I have said here makes it clear that I endorse no such thing. Critical interpretation has a standard external to itself, in the form of the world of the text. When engaged in critical interpretation we *make sense* of this world; we do not construct it. Again, the world of a work is generated by the language of the text, and so rendering explicit the constitution of a fictional world is largely a matter of linguistic interpretation. Thus we have a point of contact with the literary work, and an attendant form of interpretation, that is external to, independent of, the activity of critical interpretation. This offers us a standard against which to check critical interpretations themselves, to determine whether what the critic says is genuinely responsive to and so illuminative of his or her object of scrutiny. The activity of articulating critical meaning is not—to borrow a phrase from John McDowell—a sort of 'frictionless spinning in a void' in which nothing constrains what the reader can say about the text except the power of his or her imagination.[18] We have other forms of interpretive access to literary works which in turn function to place rational limits on critical discourse.[19]

---

[18] McDowell (1996: 11).

[19] It is here at the level of linguistic interpretation that questions arise concerning whether an interpreter simply recovers the world of a work or always partly constructs it. This is where the problem of relativism begins to appear, and I have neither the space nor the interest to pursue it here. My only claim is that critical interpretation is concerned not with constructing (or recovering) the world of a work but rather with making sense of the world once constructed (or recovered).

Before I conclude this section it is worth remarking that the picture of critical interpretation I have outlined suggests that our appreciation of literary works is much more firmly in line with our appreciation of the other arts than is often noticed—something we will fail to see if we approach literary interpretation from a purely linguistic standpoint. In most of the arts we must often use our imagination to see what an artwork wants us to see. Our ability to see a well-known actor as a certain character in a film requires an act of imaginative transformation; otherwise when viewing *A Street Car Named Desire* we would witness only Marlon Brando and never Stanley Kowalski. Or think of our ability to see a particular motion of the human body in a ballet as the movement of a swan; a stage set in the theatre as a café in the East Village; an odd configuration of cubes in a painting as a mother embracing her child. None of these viewings would be possible without the aid of the imagination. They are all distilled through an act of the imagination in a way our everyday viewings of non-artistic reality very likely are not. In most of the arts we must in some way imaginatively transform the material we are presented with if we are to encounter the world of the work. In literature it is the language that runs through the text that the imagination is to transform; in the visual arts it is commonly a perceived object. This is enough to keep the boundary between literature and the visual arts intact. But the difference between the sort of imaginative envisioning required by literature and the other arts is a matter of degree, not kind. Critical interpretation, and the form of artistic appreciation to which it is linked, would thus seem to be fairly uniform across the arts, a form of interpretation they have in common.

4.2. INTERPRETATION AND THE INVESTING OF FICTION WITH LIFE

It is quite common to take a reductively linguistic approach to the question of how literature relates to life, attempting to answer it by trying to locate literature's cognitive value in what literary works actually *say*. Among other things, an approach of this sort often results in a very awkward attempt to claim that literary works, though evidently content to speak about fictions, must also, in some roundabout way, be talking about reality. The idea of critical interpretation shows us how we might avoid such an approach, for it brings to light a way of understanding the role the interpreter—the *reader*—plays in effecting the passage from literature to life. The theory of critical interpretation outlined here allows us to accept, should we be so inclined, even a 'strong' thesis of fictionality of literary works—namely, that they *say* nothing about reality. But it also shows us that a literary work can be about much more than what it explicitly or literally says, so that, even if we embrace a strong thesis of the fictionality of literature, there still remain possibilities for claiming that literature can offer an engagement with extra-textual reality.

Without the critic, and without the reader more generally, there may be little sense to the idea that literature can bring reality to view, for without the critic's voice we find a work that seems to speak about fictions alone, thus disclosing, if anything, the imaginary rather than the real. But once we look toward the practice of criticism, we find that there is an intuitive and at any rate harmless way of speaking of literature as offering visions of life. Literature's ability to disclose reality need not consist in some mimetic act performed solely by the text. It can rather be understood to have reference to the ways in which readers imbue literary works with worldly significance. That is, the forging of a literary vision of reality is tied to this activity of placing fictions in a critical context that specifies how they are about or mean something of 'real' consequence.

Without this act of critical articulation, the passage from literature to life remains a mere potential in the literary work. In critical interpretation we enlarge, we enrich, the scope of literary experience, indeed of the literary work itself. We do so by casting fictional characters and the worlds they inhabit, not as real, but as continuous with—of a piece with—human reality. This is what we see in the examples of Eagleton on Woolf, Brooks on Faulkner, in the claims that Bartleby shows us something about modern alienation, Prospero culture and reason, Xanadu the nature of inspiration. That is, we see in these examples that the activity of articulating critical meaning reveals a process of investing fiction with life. There is nothing philosophically suspicious in saying that literature speaks about fictions yet can reveal reality, at least if we explain this not in terms of literature's magical ability to speak about two things at once—it does not have this—but rather by remarking on how the conversation that exists between literary works and interpretative practices can itself be the source of the connection between fiction and reality.

The passage from literature to life does not occur solely within the literary work (or at least we need not insist that it does if we are to give sense to humanism). It is in part a product of a stance we take towards a text, a critical stance that complements rather than conflicts with whatever 'fictive stance' we also assume towards literary content. In fact, we can find examples of literary works calling on us to assume a worldly stance. There was an interesting tradition in the history of the novel, one that seems to have vanished when modernism stepped onto the scene. It was the practice of prefacing a novel with a request, simply put, to take the fiction *seriously*. To give two well-known examples, in an author's note Fyodor Dostoevsky says the following about his *Notes from Underground*:

Both the author of these Notes and the Notes themselves are, of course, fictitious. Nevertheless, such persons as the author of these memoirs not only may, but must, exist in our society, if we take into consideration the circumstances which led to the formation of our society. It has been my wish to show the public a character of the recent past more clearly than is usually shown.[20]

And Charles Dickens writes in his preface to *Oliver Twist*:

[20] Dostoevsky (2001: 95).

It is useless to discuss whether the conduct and character of the girl seems natural or unnatural, probable or improbable, right or wrong. IT IS TRUE... It is emphatically God's truth, for it is the truth. It involves the best and worst shades of our common nature; much of its ugliest hues, and some of its most beautiful; it is a contradiction, an anomaly, an apparent impossibility, but it is a truth.[21]

We can find similar requests by Daniel Defoe, Henry Fielding, and Samuel Richardson: virtually all the first great English novelists. All of them suffered from a certain anxiety: a fear that the fictionality of their texts would lead them to be read as frivolous entertainment. Thus they found it necessary to ask their public to see in their works something the crude reader might miss: this engagement with reality that is not given explicit statement in the language of their literary creations.

Though the tradition of calling for seriousness of appreciation is now extinct, unless we are beholden to a very silly theory, we will not think that this is because we have come to learn that literature is after all just play. The reason the tradition died is probably that we, as a culture, have learned to take the novel seriously, that, whereas there was once a question about whether fictions could offer only diversion, we have learned to read aright. What these authors are denying is the appropriateness of a *merely* fictive stance, a stance that cuts our experience of literary content off from anything other than an appreciation of creatures of pure fantasy. And notice how clear these authors are in what they want us to take seriously, how precise their plea is: that we allow their works to show us something about ourselves, our cultural reality, indeed 'more clearly than is usually shown'.

If we take an absurdly narrow view of literature—a reductive stance that casts literary works as having commerce exclusively with the fantastic and the unreal simply because they tend to speak about fictions—we will not be able to take these authors at their word. But, if are willing to treat them, and our literary culture more generally,

---

[21] Dickens (2003: 22).

as voicing an implicit invitation to read our world into works of fiction, we will have no difficulty doing this. It is common, these days at least, to claim that works of literary fiction carry with them an implicit request to treat their language as prescribing imaginings. What these examples bring to light is that we have reason to see our literary practices as issuing a complementary request: we are called on to assume a critical stance that allows life to be blown into these works, a stance that in turn permits these literary works to reach a further, and intended, destination: a point of contact with our world.

It is in this respect that we see how the fictive and worldly stances we take towards literary works can come together. They do not mark opposed ways we can view some presented content (as functioning *either* to describe the real *or* to depict the fictional). They rather identify the two sides of the same appreciate attitude. Much of the time, of course, this act of reading the world into literary works is second nature, at least to anyone who has had any exposure to the practice of reading fiction (perhaps similar to our ability to see a tree, or body, in a painting that has parted with the conventions of realism: this may always require an interpretation, but of the most basic and immediate sort). It comes to us naturally, and with such ease that the distinction between interpretation and understanding is in many cases blurred. But it is interpretation, specifically the practice of criticism, that brings to view how this is done. When we examine critical discourse, when we explore the sorts of claims interpreters make of literary works, we see very clearly *that* this happens, and so just how the reader has a hand in erecting the bridge between literature and life.

One might worry that to look towards interpretation to make sense of the basic connection between literature and life is to flout what the sceptic earlier called the textual constraint: the requirement that a viable theory of humanism must show that the insight into reality we think a literary work puts on offer is a proper feature of literary content. But this is a mistake. The connection between fiction and reality is external—is *hors-texte*—in so far as it requires the presence of something external to the literary work to be made manifest—namely, our critical and interpretative activities. But this is not to say that it remains severed from literary content, that it marks a way of speaking about something other than what we witness when we look between the covers of a novel. It is better understood as a way of *filling out* literary content, of imbuing it with this general worldly relevance and thus completing the vision of reality a work wishes to put on offer. Again, critical interpretation marks a way of articulating what the world of a work *means*. In this respect, the critical meanings we attribute to literary works become bound up with our understanding of the content of these works, of what they are about. Thus the connection between fiction and reality achieved in our critical activities never remains wholly external to the work. Indeed, if interpretation struggles to specify what a literary work is *about*, then it is by that fact a specification of a feature of literary content.

4.3. CRITICISM AND COGNITIVISM

What this discussion of interpretation helps us to see is that the range of literary aboutness extends beyond the fictional and into the real. This, in turn, gives sense to basic humanist claim that we can see reality in literary works while all the while knowing that the particulars they hold up for view are creatures of the imagination. But it also opens up an interesting respect in which we can see our literary practice as generative of something of quite obvious cognitive value. Seeing this will allow me to complete the story I have been telling in this book of how our literary practices play a central role in our various attempts to give sense to our world.

As before, the sort of cognitive value I shall link to our critical practices will make no reference to the acquisition of so-called propositional knowledge, which is the sort of cognitive value often thought to be at stake here. Rather, what I want to suggest is that critical interpretation plays a role in what we might call *the articulation of culture*, which I take to be quite different from proffering the standard sorts of knowledge. By calling on us to ascribe meaning to the range of human activities and experiences a novel brings to critical attention, literature plays an important role in the expansion and refinement of our understanding of social and cultural reality. We may not get truths, properly so called, from this, but we get something just as important from the worldly point of view: the bestowal of sense, of meaning, upon those regions of human circumstance that literature invites us to explore. Let me explain.

Recall that one power we habitually ascribe to literary works in non-philosophical contexts—a power the argument of the previous section permits us to invoke—is its capacity to bring life to view in all of its varied complexity. That is, we find a complexity of *vision*, a finely textured presentation of human activity and circumstance. In this respect, the process of giving sense to literary content requires working through a work that calls on us to explore life at a level of detail and precision that our less dramatic encounters with our world rarely afford. Since the visions of life we are put in touch with in literary experience are typically so complex, so rich in detail and texture, they very often have the air of *novelty*: we see in them something not quite seen before. This is not to say that, whenever we come upon a literary work, we see a form of human activity or experience hitherto unknown to us. This is surely too strong. Rather, our sense of the complexity of these visions resides largely in the fact that, as much as we might recognize familiar aspects of human life in literary worlds—our everyday emotional, moral, social, and similar practices and experiences—we find that in literature these already known regions of reality tend to suggest deeper layers of meaning and hint at broader patterns of aboutness and significance. When placed in the context of a literary work, these regions of our world commonly say, as Umberto Eco puts it, 'I mean more'—more, at any rate, than we had once thought.[22] Accordingly, critics, if they

---

[22] Eco (1994: 27).

are to conquer this complexity, must struggle to give voice to these more profound reserves of meaning and aboutness literature reveals our characteristically human practices to store.

So here is the question I think we must ask if we are to address the cognitive value of our literary-critical practices: what is the value of having a textual tradition that presents to appreciation such complex visions of life, and of having a critical practice that struggles to articulate their meaning? That is, what does a culture acquire in respect of its ability to give meaning, sense, to its world in virtue of this activity? To answer this question, simply consider the value—and here I mean cognitive value—of a practice that involves us in the process of expanding our capacity to speak about human reality, of producing richer possibilities for investing it with meaning and significance. I think the response we should want to give is that the conversation that exists between literary works and our critical practices is one of the mechanisms by which a culture articulates a sense of its world, and thus that literary works and our critical traditions are mutually implicated in a practice that itself bears cognitive value. To confer meaning upon something is to make it available to thought: it is to create sense, and thus understanding, where there once was none. And, if our literary-critical practices have a role to play in fleshing out our sense of human culture—of the meaning, of the significance, of various human practices and experiences—it would seem that they also have a rather important role to play in the expansion and refinement of our understanding of our shared world.

It is occasionally important to recall that, at least once upon a time, we were rather dumb animals, without much of substance to say about the nature of our world. Literary works in tandem with our critical practices represent a culture's search for—to borrow a phrase from Richard Eldridge—'expressive freedom'.[23] That is, they represent our struggle to find ever more adequate ways of rendering

---

[23] See Eldridge (1997), especially the chapter 'Wittgenstein's Writerliness and its Repressions', for a discussion of this idea.

explicit what we take our world to be. By presenting to us visions of life upon which we build more refined understandings of our way in the world, literature functions to expand the boundaries of what we can say about our world and our particular ways of finding ourselves in it. It is an activity, in short, that has a valuable role to play in the evolution of our expressive and conceptual access to reality.

On this picture our critical encounters with literature do not offer truth, at least not in the standard philosophical sense of the term. It would seem to be the philosopher's rather than the literary critic's business (or perhaps interest) to explore the literary visions of life and ask whether they are also true, whether our world is *really* like that. The cognitive value of our critical practices resides not in the deliverance of truth, but in the production and attempt to give sense to these visions themselves. We might call the sort of understanding our critical practices gives us 'cultural' understanding: understanding of how we give meaning to various regions of human circumstance. But this is not thereby to assign a worrisomely inferior status to these visions. Indeed, this activity enjoys a certain priority to the search for truth and knowledge, at least, and perhaps only, in this respect: before we can query the truth of a vision of our way in the world, we must first have the vision itself. That is, what makes possible the search for truth is a prior cultural accomplishment: the construction of varying ways of taking our world to be. As I argued in the previous chapter, if we want to show that we can treat our encounters with literature as having cognitive value, it should be enough to show that they engage us in the activity of trying to articulate an understanding of our way in the world.

In conclusion, let me offer a word about the solitary reader, who may seem to have been ignored in all this. Most readers, after all, do not play a very significant role in our critical practices. But there is no reason to think that the story I have just told about our critical practices cannot be retold on the level of an individual's private encounters with literary works. What I find of such interest in our critical practices is precisely that they are public, that they constitute a discipline, and thus are suited, in a way the solitary reader is not, to play a significant role in the general story I have been telling in this book of how literary works act as communal storehouses of sorts in which we place the various stories we have to tell of ourselves and our world. In the previous two chapters I have discussed how literary works function as archives of this sort. What I hope to have shown here is that the works that constitute our critical traditions can be seen as constituting a complementary archive. Our private encounters with literary works, since private, will not play a central role in the construction of these archives. But perhaps this is too dismissive of solitary readers, for they, along with critics, booksellers, publishers, and many more in addition, make up that broad constellation of practices that is the institution of literature. All have a role to play in this instruction, the critic as well as the lone reader.

5

The Fictional and the Real

I have given my arguments for literary humanism. With the conclusion of the previous chapter I have completed what I hope to be a plausible model for understanding the two basic ideas to which a viable theory of literary humanism must give sense: that we can see our world in literature and that this seeing is cognitively significant. What I would like to do in this final chapter is relax the discussion a bit and offer some general observations on the notion of fiction.

I shall use a discussion of two positions from extreme corners of currently fashionable theories of fiction as an occasion for these reflections. The positions I have in mind are poststructuralist antirealism or 'textualism' and the 'mimesis as make-believe' theory that is so influential in analytical aesthetics. I choose them because I take them to be excellent representatives of two popular ways of approaching the relationship between reality and fiction: the 'radical' one of dismissing the distinction altogether and the 'conservative' one of accepting it wholeheartedly and then going on to contrast them such that fiction is turned into an imaginary version of the *real* world. Neither theory is particularly hospitable to the literary humanist. Without the distinction between reality and fiction, the humanist loses the basic terms of his theory; and, if the appreciation of works of fiction is just a game of make-believe, it seems we have to say that we *pretend* to see, rather than actually *do* see, our world in literature.

What we will gain from this discussion is an idea of where the theory of humanism I have developed in this book sits within the spectrum of currently marketed moves in theories of fiction. In explaining why these two approaches are inadequate, I also hope to bring into view a few basic constraints on how to explain what we are saying when we describe a work of literature as fictional. I will conclude with a call to 'openness' in the theory of fiction—that is, with an invitation to explore the various ways in which the frame of the fictional can be, or should be, understood to keep open a window on the real. In making a case for this, I will look at a few non-literary practices that routinely enlist fictions in their pursuit of reality, with the hope of casting light on the general humanistic and intellectual functions we assign fictions in our cultural practices.

5.1. THE THREAT OF PANFICTIONALISM

If any current philosophical or literary-critical argument has made its way from university classrooms and into the consciousness of the educated public at large, it is the argument for what I will call panfictionalism,[1] the thesis, to put it roughly at first mention, that all forms of discourse are at the end of the day alike in being forms of fictional discourse. It might best be described, or so I shall suggest, as a ghost argument, for I am not sure that the theorists held responsible for panfictionalism promote it in a way that would make it a genuine threat. It has become a bit of a bogeyman at any rate, and so it is fitting to say a few words about it.

To state something obvious but rarely acknowledged by those who believe panfictionalism to be an import shipped solely out of the Left Bank, positions that might fairly, if loosely, be called panfictionalist have enjoyed currency in both contemporary literary theory and philosophy, on both sides of the ocean, endorsed in one form or another by philosophers and critics as diverse as Nelson Goodman

---

[1] The term 'panfictionalism' is not standard. I take it, I believe, from Lubomír Doležel, though I am unfortunately unsure of the source of this term.

and Jean-François Lyotard.² One respect in which some prominent areas of Anglo-American philosophy and continental theory have overlapped is in denying that there is a sustainable distinction between what is made up and what is discovered, between the bits of the known world that are culturally constructed and discourse dependent and those that are just 'out there' and free of all linguistic and cultural trappings. This is hardly a new claim, if we keep the history of anti-realism in mind. But certain contemporary literary and philosophical movements have developed it in such a way that this old position seems to have been given new clothing. I have in mind here panfictionalism as we find it especially in French and North American poststructuralism and postmodernism, the region of current 'theory' with which we often contrast (helpfully or not) analytical philosophy.

In its most notorious and arguably excessive form, we have the wing of postmodernism typified by the later writings of Jean Baudrillard. To gloss a familiar position, Baudrillard has popularized the idea that in our age reality has been lost and replaced with 'hyperreality'. We live under the tyranny of what he calls *simulacra*, a sort of cyberworld in which symbols have overtaken the symbolized and in so doing banished the reality our linguistic signs once stood for.³ Baudrillard's postmodernism, and the school of thought associated with it, might playfully be described as what we would have if Marshall McLuhan had written Don Dellilo's *White Noise*, the belief that media has usurped message sung as a dirge for contemporary culture. A characteristic claim might be:

Disneyland is there to conceal the fact that it is the 'real' country, all of 'real' America, which is Disneyland . . . Disneyland is presented as imaginary in order to make us believe that the rest is real, when in fact all of Los Angeles

---

² If one has difficulty seeing why Goodman would be included in this list, his idea that we have not *a* world but world versions, and even more basically his idea that worlds are made, not found, is the reason for his inclusion in this group. See Goodman (1978).

³ See, e.g., Baudrillard (1983*a*).

and the America surrounding it are no longer real, but of the order of the hyperreal and simulation.[4]

If we generalize Baudrillard's musing on Disneyland into a description of contemporary culture at large, we have what we might call the 'pop' version of panfictionalism, the territory of contemporary theory that is probably responsible for the fact that so many analytic philosophers are unwilling to take seriously anything that goes by the name of 'postmodernism' or 'poststructuralism'.

What we might call 'proper' panfictionalism, the form of panfictionalism I am interested in here, comes from another corner of postmodern/poststructuralist thought, and it is none too difficult to pinpoint exactly which. When we find on the back cover of one of the most prominent contemporary works of analytic literary aesthetics blurbs such as 'The establishment has been sitting like a rabbit for too long in the headlights of literary theory', and 'An excellent and accessible account of fiction, which is used to dissect the pretension of postmodernist literary theory', we just *know*, even if no names are mentioned, whom the authors have in mind.[5] It is the area of theory that is identified not with Baudrillarian 'pop' panfictionalism but most conspicuously with Derrida and Paul de Man (and the so-called Yale School), that very academically active form of deconstruction-inspired philosophy and criticism that dominated North American departments of literature from the 1970s to the 1990s and that continues to exert tremendous influence.

The basic form of the threat they supposedly pose is thought to lie in their taking philosophy's core distinctions between fact and fiction, truth and falsity, referring expression and referent, and deconstructing them into oblivion, attempting to pull out from beneath us the traditional foundation upon which investigations into the nature of literary-fictive writing have been built.[6] Terry Eagleton

---

[4] Baudrillard (1983*b*: 25).

[5] The book is Lamarque and Olsen's *Truth, Fiction and Literature* (1994), and the blurbs are from Richard Gaskin and David Novitz, respectively.

[6] See Searle (1993) for a characteristic voicing of the threat this wing of poststructuralism is thought to pose.

captures as well as one could want the basic form of panfictionalism with which these theorists are thought to threaten us.

> It is a mistake to believe that any language is *literally* literal. Philosophy, law, political theory work by metaphor just as poems do, and so are just as fictional . . . literature for the deconstructionists testifies to the impossibility of language ever doing more than talk about its own failure, like some barroom bore. Literature is the ruin of all reference, the cemetery of communication.[7]

And Stanley Fish might also be mentioned here:

> When we communicate, it is because we are parties to a set of discourse agreements which are in effect decisions as to what can be stipulated as fact. It is these decisions and the agreement to abide by them, rather than the availability of substance, that make it possible for us to refer, whether we are novelists or reporters for the *New York Times*. One might object that this has the consequence of making all discourse fictional; but it would be just as accurate to say that it makes all discourse serious, and it would be better still to say that it puts all discourse on a par.[8]

Unlike Baudrillardian 'pop' panfictionalism—which, as even the sympathetic often concede, tends to trade in sweeping pronouncements elicited from rather flighty critical observations[9]—in its highest form deconstruction (and related forms of poststructuralism) bases its panfictionalism on the detailed scrutiny of concrete texts, arguably as a radicalized appropriation of New Criticism's method of 'close reading'. And the fear concerns what these theorists seem to be claiming to have discovered from their readings: that all forms of writing are equally fictional.[10]

---

[7] Eagleton (1997: 145–6).   [8] Fish (1980: 244–3).

[9] For example, see the discussions of Baudrillard in Best and Kellner (1991); McHale (1992); Selden and Widdowson (1993); and Bertens (1995).

[10] It is for something like this reason we find these dictums in poststructuralist literary theory: Derrida's claim that putatively literal or nonfictional texts are 'those in which the metaphor has been forgotten' (Derrida 1976: 34), Christopher Norris's claim that 'literary texts are less deluded than the discourse of philosophy' (Norris 1982: 21), and de Man's curiously apocalyptic proclamation that 'philosophy turns out to be an endless reflection on its own destruction at the hands of literature' (de Man 1979: 115).

The perceived threat is that it seems that proper panfictionalists want to claim that every writer who has based his investigation into literature on the assumption of the uniqueness of works of fiction is seriously misguided. Indeed, it *looks* like the thesis of panfictionalism is simply claiming that there is *no* justification for making a basic contrast, as I have throughout this book, between world-constructing and world-imaging texts. The implication appears to be that the entire frame of the debate in which our humanist engages is irreparably damaged, to be thrown aside. For, if every form of discourse has the logic of fictional discourse, if all can be reduced to imaginative construction, to narratives woven creatively and not by objective discovery, then the humanist must be misguided, block-headed really, since the distinction on which he bases his investigation is metaphysically mute.

Or so it would seem. But let us take a step back. Clearly (and as we saw in the discussion of the poststructuralist drift in Chapter 1) there is a threat to a great number of core philosophical ideas here, from the notion that facts and fictions enjoy a different metaphysical status to the possibility of extra-linguistic reference. From here it is tempting to make the leap to the conclusion that panfictionalism implies that there is *nothing* of substance in the distinction between literary fiction and works of non-fiction, between texts that function to depict our world and those that generate fictional worlds. The question is whether this conclusion is warranted. I will call this the *no-difference thesis*, and I shall treat it as claiming that the position described above destroys without remainder any theory of literary fiction that takes seriously the distinction between works of fiction and non-fiction. As we will see, it is only the no-difference thesis that poses a genuine threat to this distinction. And that panfictionalism does not imply this thesis is very easy to show.

Now, if we wanted, here we could rehearse standard anti-sceptical arguments we often find in philosophy and attempt to tackle the issue by trying to undermine the panfictionalist's ability to make wholesale claims to the effect that language fails to connect us to reality (as would appear to underlie the claim that all discourse is 'fictional'). But the argument I have in mind is not so technical. In fact, it is altogether pedestrian, and I think effective for this reason. It recommends itself without requiring any stance towards the thesis of panfictionalism, and so it can be accepted regardless of where one stands in relation to the line that divides the radicals from the conservatives in this debate.

The basic idea is this: while—let us say for the sake of argument—there may be any number of interesting respects in which it is possible to collapse the fact/fiction distinction, *within* the practice of *reading* various texts it makes all the difference whether or not we read something as fiction or non-fiction. That is, regardless of whether the objects of each type of text turn out, on metaphysical reflection, to be fictitious, we can still give solid ground to the distinction. The question is social, a matter of what sort of attitude is called on by the practice, cultural at root, of appreciating a work *as a work of fiction*.[11]

I begin only with the assumption, quite uncontroversial I would think, that, if I present you with a text and tell you that it is a work of literary fiction, you would not read it in the same way you would if I presented it to you as (and convinced you that it was) non-fiction, regardless of whether you are a wild panfictionalist or a rigid realist. And from this I think it is a very easy step to see that we explain this by stating that it is because you know, if you at all understand the practices of reading fiction and non-fiction, that, while one sort of texts asks to be read as attempting to describe our world, the other does not.

It is irrelevant to the distinction between fiction and non-fiction whether all narratives—historical, philosophical, literary—are equally 'made-up', groundless. If we embrace panfictionalism, we will believe that those texts that feign to represent the world will always fail to give us what they promise. But notice that we can speak

---

[11] In making this argument I am indebted to and build upon similar arguments first developed by Walton (1990: esp. ch. 2) and Lamarque and Olsen (1994: esp. chs. 2 and 7).

of *failure* here, that we can say that they are deluded in believing that they can aspire to show us reality. And it is revealing that we would never say that a literary text *fails* in this respect, for the reason that we do not even treat works of literary fiction as having this aspiration, that we do not regard them as players in this sort of game. This supports what has been repeated throughout this book: while we use, generally put, the criterion of adequacy to 'the way the world is' when evaluating standard forms of non-fiction, we do not when evaluating literary fiction. Panfictionalism may offer reasons for rejecting the traditional ways in which we explain this notion of adequacy (we lose, among other things, the concepts of truth, correspondence to the facts, reference to extra-textual reality), but it in no obvious way tells us that there is no interesting distinction to be made between the structure of appreciation and logic of evaluation we apply to the writings we find in *Scientific American* and *Granta*. Regardless of whether we accept or reject panfictionalism, we are beginning to see that we still have a way to maintain a distinction between how different sorts of texts attempt to relate us to the world.

The point is so transparent that one finds oneself with a red face in stating it. Need it be said, even if one regards works of history and science as both teeming with fictions, if one *reads* them as one reads a work of literary fiction, one would be engaging in a glaring act of cultural incompetence. For this is the best we could say of someone who, when discussing his culture, does not or cannot distinguish the world he finds in Orwell's *1984* from the one he learns about in his twentieth-century history course in university. And, when we explain this incompetence, in no obvious sense do we need to invoke a theory of facts and fictions, or any theory at all. It is not because of a particular *theory* of the possibility, say, of extra-textual reference that we can say that, while a *Rough Guide* travel book speaks about the 'real' Venice and Cyprus, *Othello* describes fictional versions of the same locations. It is to say that, while in the first case the text is read as trying to depict particulars and happenings found in the actual world, in the second it is not.

This point will be given some strength in the next section, but the claim at hand is that each brick in the wall that separates fiction from non-fiction can be accounted for in broadly pragmatic terms, in terms of the different ways we put sorts of text to use. In accounting for this we do not need to enlist a metaphysical vocabulary but the vocabulary of a convention-based practice—what we might describe as the socially prescribed rules of reading.[12] Once we see that the contrast can be explained on the level of convention, the type of reflections panfictionalism offers do nothing to threaten the basic distinction between fiction and non-fiction. As Doležel notes: 'if reality is called fiction, a new word for fiction has to be invented.'[13] In other words, even if we accept panfictionalism, at best we will find ourselves with a contrast between texts we take to offer fictional worlds and those we take to offer representations of *our* 'fictional' reality. We will still have justification for believing in the uniqueness of literary fiction.

It may be the case, let us concede for the moment, that what we call 'reality' or a 'fact' are just fictions to which we have allotted special privileges in our language games. But, if this is so, without a tremendous amount of additional argumentation, claims of this order in no way suggest that we should regard literary fiction and non-fiction as both pointing the reader in the same direction, towards the worlds of narrative fiction. The reordering of our metaphysical assumptions about the nature of reality may cause shifts in what we understand to be the objects of straightforwardly empirical descriptions, but it will not in any conceivable way remove the wall we place between Captain Ahab's world and ours. If we take the metaphysical substance out of our understanding of the difference between these two worlds, we are left with the very thick residue of conventional distinction, thick enough to show that a great space

---

[12] As Lamarque and Olsen put it, 'the fictive dimension of stories (or narratives) is explicable only in terms of a rule-governed practice, central to which are a certain mode of utterance (fictive utterance) and a certain complex of attitudes (the fictive stance)' (Lamarque and Olsen 1994: 32).

[13] Doležel (1998: p. x).

still exists between the two. And this reveals the no-difference thesis to be indefensible.

Panfictionalism tells us what counts as fictional—everything—but not what counts as a work of *literary* fiction. It makes a claim about when narratives describe fictitious objects—always—but not when they are narratives of *fictional worlds*. Panfictionalism does not suggest that philosophical honesty calls on us to remove the Fiction and Non-fiction designators we find in bookstores. To be sure, the distinction is no more challenged by the sort of theoretical observations panfictionalism offers than the everyday distinction between past and present is by the theory of relativity or McTaggart's Paradox. If McTaggart was right, we will need to change the theory with which we explain the practice of using this distinction. But we would not say that the distinction is to be completely abandoned, as though we would think someone a great fool should he still distinguish his past from his present. Likewise, panfictionalism at best threatens what we believe to be the available range of theories for explaining certain routine ways of contrasting the kinds of objects described in works of fiction and non-fiction. It does not threaten the distinction itself.

I think we can see the bogeyman. For panfictionalism to be any sort of threat to the *literary* distinction between fiction and non-fiction, it must amount to a no-difference thesis. But this is clearly false, as alluring as the inference might be when we find a literary theorist or philosopher arguing that ultimately every form of discourse succeeds no more than narrative fiction in describing non-discursive reality. It is an interesting question for metaphysics, semantics, and discourse theory, but not for the attempt to defend literary humanism.

In fact, as it is promoted by those who are considered a threat, panfictionalism is almost always presented on either metaphysical or semantic/linguistic grounds, a theory whose point is to deflate the claim, for example, that philosophy and science are more sophisticated than literature because they attempt to get outside their own textuality and touch reality. It is a sign of the blurring distinction between the work done by philosophers and literary theorists that literary theorists, under the guidance of Derrida and a few others, are entering into this debate, not an indication that they have hijacked core philosophical notions and used them to wreak havoc on our common-sense notions of the different ways works of fiction and non-fiction engage our appreciation. Indeed, as far as I can tell, panfictionalism is the old dish of anti-realism served up by literary theorists and 'continental' thinkers, perhaps seasoned differently from what more earthbound philosophers might be used to, but essentially a contemporary version of a very ancient plate—and no more relevant to issues of the distinction between different types of texts than anti-realism has ever been.[14]

There is an optimistic upshot of panfictionalism, and we should notice this before closing this discussion, since I believe that any humanist should take it to heart. 'Proper' or Derrida/Yale School-inspired panfictionalism, as I understand it, is essentially used as a foil against the literarily crude but still prevalent idea that, because works of literary fiction are 'made-up', they are at best charming playthings: entertaining but ultimately empty texts that are to be set aside from the cognitively valuable writings of philosophy and the hard and soft sciences. In other words, proper panfictionalism is in part motivated by the desire to undermine traditional reasons for denying literature the status of the serious, reasons that since Plato have led many philosophers to dismiss literature as often beautiful and amusing but basically trivial. I would venture that this explains much of the allure panfictionalism has for the serious admirer of literature. This motivation to restore dignity to literature in the face of the charge that its fictionality makes it frivolous is admirable, a desire that also motivates the attempt to do justice to the intuitions of the literary humanist.

Nevertheless, we do seem to pay an extremely high philosophical price for this. And I think that, in paying this fee, we find that we get what we want much too cheaply. We put literature on a par with other forms of writing by vulgarizing the competition,

---

[14] See Rorty, 'Nineteenth–Century Idealism and Twentieth–Century Textualism', in Rorty (1982) for a convincing discussion of this.

making every form of writing have the same flaw that is traditionally used to deny literature membership among the serious forms of writing. What we should rather try to show, as our humanist has, is that literature can be seen as having an equal claim to bringing us into contact with what the putative 'heavy' forms of writing do. It is hard to imagine anyone sympathetic to humanism accepting panfictionalism for this reason, and I hope the arguments I have given for humanism in the previous chapters make clear how far from this aspect of panfictionalism our humanist stands. The authors who have given us 'proper' panfictionalism have been invaluable for forcing into the debate a re-evaluation of the idea of literature as somehow a 'non-serious' form of writing. But we would do best not to adopt their precise strategy for undermining anti-literary prejudices.

5.2. THE LIMITS OF MAKE-BELIEF

If poststructuralism has swept through literature departments, the theory I shall discuss here has, at least since the 1990 publication of Kendall Walton's *Mimesis as Make-Believe*, been the dominant model of fiction in analytical aesthetics. I discussed it in broad outline in Chapter 1 when I went over the analytic drift, and here I want to add a few more observations to make clear why I do not think the make-believe theory can be reconciled either with an understanding of how we appreciate literary *works* or with the demands of an adequate theory of literary humanism.

Before beginning, I should make it clear that I shall be using a very precise, or what I shall occasionally refer to as *canonical*, sense of 'make-believe'. The term 'make-believe' is used widely and loosely in aesthetics, often interchangeably with the fairly neutral and much weaker 'imagination'. I have nothing against this looser sense of make-believe, and nothing I say here should be taken to suggest that I think literary aesthetics would do well to rid itself of all talk of make-believe. The theorists who put forward the canonical account of make-believe cast make-believe as a matter of imagining the descriptions that run through a literary work to be *true*, and thus that we make-believe, in a sense I shall soon specify, the fictional world of a literary work to be *real*. It is this idea of pretending fictions to be real, fictional content to be true, that I shall take issue with. I am sure that at times we do this, and at any rate I cannot imagine why one should deny that we do. The danger is the common identification of make-believe in this canonical sense with the *basic* imaginative stance we take toward the content—*all of it*—of works of literary fiction. This is the target of the following criticisms.

Let me begin with a little scene setting. I think it fair to say that philosophical interest in the theory of fiction in analytical philosophy initially grew not out of a great interest in literary aesthetics but out of one of the mainstays of twentieth-century philosophy of language: the problem of truth and reference. As they passed from Frege and Russell onwards, studies in these areas reintroduced the problem of fiction to contemporary philosophy (or rather gave it the centrality it had been enjoying in continental phenomenology since the mid-nineteenth century). The basic issue is the trouble of 'non-referring descriptions'. It is found in a great variety of cases of reference, from counterfactual and hypothetical claims to assertions about the past, but is arguably best exemplified by the puzzle of talk about fictional objects.[15]

The insight that leads to many of the current trends in the theory of fiction is that traditional empiricist tendencies to make correspondence to reality the basic ingredient of meaningfulness yield very unsatisfactory theories of the logic and structure of fictional discourse. For obvious reasons, we will run into great difficulty when we encounter propositions with fictional content if we are beholden to a model of language that tells us (for example) that sentences derive their meaningfulness from their truth conditions, and that

---

[15] For a clear and engaging overview of contemporary theories of fiction, see Davies, in Gaut and Lopes (2001).

truth conditions are explained in terms of relations of correspondence between sentences and actual states of affairs. A frame of this sort will at best give us very crude tools for speaking about fictional content, as Russell, again, made very clear when he argued that sentences describing Hamlet 'are all false because there was no such man'.[16] Clearly this is unacceptable. If a theory of reference forces us to group every sentence that does not correspond to reality under the heading of the false, we end up with a position that implies that a fictional narrative is linguistically on a par with fibs and falsifications, as though reading a novel is not unlike receiving erroneous travel directions or being told one's horoscope.

Moreover, and more irritating to our intuitions about literature, it just cannot be right to say that the proposition 'Hamlet was mad' is *false*. With the work of Shakespeare in hand as a justification, we seem to have a very good reason for believing it, for *his* Hamlet certainly was mad. Of course, the sentence 'Hamlet was mad' is not true of the *actual* world, since Shakespeare's Hamlet was never a resident of it. But surely this sentence enjoys a *kind* of truth, however deviant its particular brand of truth may be. We know that it will not be an empirical truth; but we are in possession of an inadequate theory if for this reason we have to call it a *falsehood*. By the 1950s we see a significant amount of philosophical work put to showing fiction to have a logic that is independent of standard descriptive and 'empirical' speech.[17] The developments in theories of language—the various distinctions between meaning and use, between assertion and pretence, theories of speech acts and illocutionary acts—were carried out at least partly in response to counter-intuitive claims forced on us by the models of reference inherited from the first half of the last century.

The representatives of the make-believe movement often take as their first step in this debate the denial that the property of

---

[16] Russell (1962: 277).
[17] Most notably, the work of philosophers such as Monroe Beardsley, John Hospers, Arnold Isenberg, and Margaret MacDonald. The collection of articles in Barrett (1965) includes many of the seminal articles written on this subject in the 1950s.

'being fictional' is a semantic property.[18] The step is essential. The basic insight is that questions of a sentence's truth value cannot distinguish between the false and the fictional, as we might have noticed in Russell's infelicitous comment on *Hamlet*. They cannot distinguish between a text that is not true of reality because it is just *wrong* (say Aristotle's theory of substance in the *Metaphysics*) and one that is not because it is a work of fiction.

In fact, semantic properties cannot even distinguish the *true* from the fictional. We might imagine that the entirety of a science-fiction novel will eventually come to have the property of being true-of-the-world, in the sense that the future, by a grand act of chance, will unfold just as it does in the latest *Star Trek* novel. But, if so, we would not then say that, while it was once a work of science fiction, it has suddenly transformed itself into a historical work; as Gregory Currie quips: 'It makes good sense to ask when a work was popular, but it would be bizarre to ask when it was fictional.'[19] We would rather have a reason for asserting that what makes a literary work fictional does not reside in the truth value of the sentences of which a work of literature is composed. (If a less unlikely example is desired, think for a moment of a New Journalist novel like Truman Capote's *In Cold Blood* or the general genre of the historical novel, examples of works of literary fiction whose content is often, and intentionally, true of the world.) In short, that a text is fictional is not explicable in terms of semantic properties, for

---

[18] This is not to say that fictional sentences have no semantic relations or properties, of course. Once we fix the 'universe of discourse' of a literary fiction, we can speak of it as referring to or stating truths about objects and events in this universe (the words of *Hamlet*, in other words, can state facts about Hamlet). Thus the above argument is also not the same as arguing that we cannot have a semantic theory of *fictional reference*, which many possible worlds theorists of fiction offer. Should it be worth saying, the idea is that questions of *worldly* truth, reference, and representation will not determine fictionality. This is compatible with the claim that we can account for the fictional world a novel creates by describing how the sentences that make up a literary narrative refer to or otherwise represent the world of that text. Pavel (1986), Eco (1990: ch. 4), and Doležel (1998) have offered influential accounts of this. I gave an overview of this strategy in Section 1.3.

[19] Currie (1990: 11).

semantic properties are incapable of identifying what makes a work *a work of fiction.*

The question then becomes: what makes a work fictional if we cannot account for this in terms of the relation between the language of the text and the world? One of the great virtues of the work of the make-believe theorists is that they have done much to show that what makes a sentence or a text fictional is to be explicated socially, in terms of a practice (or a 'game') rather than in terms of linguistic and semantic categories. We capture the independence of fiction from questions of a sentence's relation to reality by describing a practice that mandates certain rules of reading, introducing certain attitudes of appreciation, and barring others. It is an insight that mirrors in many ways the move from the semantic to the social in many prominent theories of meaning, and its results are often similar.[20] If the concepts of truth and reference cannot explain what it means to be fictional, we relocate fictionality to the category of cultural convention and practice. As Lamarque and Olsen argue, the invocation of practice and convention

> Serves to emphasize that fiction is grounded in activities of a certain kind not, for example, relations of a certain kind (e.g. between language and the world). Second, it requires that this grounding be social (rather than, say, psychological) at least in the sense that works of fiction can only be given this role in a social context. Finally, there are normative implications; there are right and wrong ways of engaging in the practice.[21]

So far, so good. I would think that anyone who reads the popular statements of the make-believe theory will find that their compelling accounts of the social basis of fiction justify the amount of time one must put into reading their typically very lengthy books.

So how do we explain this practice? What is the precise attitude it tells us we bring to a work of fiction? The name of the theory

---

[20] Say in the philosophy of the later Wittgenstein, or in the move from truth conditions to assertibility conditions that characterizes many social theories of meaning.
[21] Lamarque and Olsen (1994: 34).

gives it away: the fictive stance is primarily a matter of making-believe the content of works of literary fiction. For the make-believe theorist, the fictive stance essentially consists in treating works of fiction as prescribing make-beliefs, imaginings. We might consider an example here, one that follows the standard form make-believe theorists use to illustrate this idea. Imagine a boy playing 'army', call him Little McCarthy. In his house he finds an old army field jacket, on the lapel of which are inscribed his father's rank and family name. Though the name and rank designate the father and not the boy, once the boy puts on the jacket and begins to play, they take on the role of props in a game of make-believe. In the context of the child's game, the words on the jacket are given the role of making it 'fictional' or 'make-believe' (the two are interchangeable) that the boy is General McCarthy: they generate this fictional state of affairs. Likewise, the words and descriptions we find in a literary work are to be read as projecting a make-believe world by prescribing imaginings, make-beliefs. The words that make up a work of fiction have in their standard or primary use the function of designating and describing real objects and actual states of affairs (as the written name and rank on McCarthy's field jacket do). But, once placed under the scope of an attitude of make-belief, they take on the role of describing 'facts' about a world of make-believe, generating fictional truths about its contours. As Currie puts it:

When we read and become absorbed by a work of fiction we may find compelling images before our minds, but a work of history or a newspaper article can stimulate the imagination in the same way. What distinguishes reading fiction from the reading of non-fiction is not the activity of the imagination but the attitude we adopt toward the content of what we read: make-belief in one case, belief in the other.[22]

We should also consider Walton's seminal passage:

In order to understand paintings, plays, films, and novels, we must first look at dolls, hobbyhorses, toy trucks, and teddy bears. The activities in which

[22] Currie (1990: 21).

representational works of art are embedded and which give them their point are best seen as continuous with children's games of make-believe. Indeed, I advocate regarding these activities as games of make-believe themselves, and I shall argue that representational works function as props in such games, as dolls and teddy bears serve as props in children's games.[23]

It is important to see that, for the canonical make-believe theorist, make-believe is not only an attitude we take towards the particular sentences in a text that we know to be false of the world. It is a *comprehensive* attitude used to preface, as it were, our involvement with the entirety of a novel. Of course, the make-believe theorist *must* claim this, for the sake of consistency. Otherwise the theory would fail to be a theory of the stance we take towards fictional *works*, since without this stipulation it would function only to explain our attitude towards those sentences occurring in a literary work that are not true of the world, thus leaving the many accurate geographical, historical, psychological (and so on) descriptions we find in literary works unaccounted for. Since virtually every work of literature has many such descriptions, this would amount to a failure to offer a theory of what it means for something to be a work of fiction and instead reveal itself to be just a theory of fictional sentences. Indeed, it would amount to a reintroduction of the semantic theory of fiction, implying as it would that whether something is a fiction is determined by its failure to be true of or to correspond to reality. Thus we subsume a *work* under the fictive stance, described as a rule-governed attitude that has the implicit form of 'it is fictional that " . . . " ' (which is translatable into 'it is make-believe that " . . . " '[24]), with ' . . . ' filled in with the content of a literary narrative or propositions descriptive of literary content.

---

[23] Walton (1990: 11).
[24] It is difficult to find make-believe theorists who agree on the precise translation schema. The nuances between, for example, 'it is make-believe that', 'it is make-believe true that', or ' " . . . " is true in a game of make-believe' turn out to be quite significant, depending on other theoretical commitments. Currie (1990) explains well the challenges of finding an intuitive translation schema.

It is easy to see why a philosopher would find the make-believe theory so attractive. If we once felt that, as much as it cannot be *false* that Hamlet was mad, it nevertheless cannot quite be *true*, the make-believe theory offers us a logically tidy way of making sense of this. If we once thought that neither belief nor disbelief can quite capture our attitude towards fictional content, the make-believe theory provides an elegant remedy. My concession that it is not properly *true* that Hamlet was mad (he never *was*, so he never was mad) does not imply, as Russell seemed to think, that this proposition is false. It is *fictionally* true, a proposition that describes an imagining prescribed by the text of *Hamlet*. If we do not believe that *Othello* lived in Venice (for he never lived at all), we are no longer forced to concede that we therefore disbelieve it. We neither believe nor disbelieve it: we *make*-believe it.

If evaluated from the vantage point of twentieth-century analytical philosophy of language, the make-believe theory is very impressive. Given their philosophical endowment, it represents a huge improvement over many of the earlier theories of fiction and fiction-making. For this reason I doubt that anyone who has tried to trace the history of the theory of fiction will fail to appreciate how much the make-believe theorists have raised the bar in the debate on the nature of fiction. And, lest it seem that in the following I bite the hand that has been feeding me, there is much of this that I have made use of in prior discussions and to which my own theory is indebted.

However, the theory does have a tendency to overextend itself. The problem concerns the comprehensiveness of the attitude it asks us to bring to literature—namely, the extent to which it claims that make-believe expresses our basic orientation towards literary content (indeed towards all the 'representational arts', as Walton develops it). As we just saw, the make-believe theorist's account of the fictional operator does not only subsume a text's non-referring (or patently false-of-the-world) sentences under its scope; it enlists the entire content of a literary narrative in its game of make-believe. But we also just saw—and as we surely knew without being reminded of it—that literary content is often world-adequate, which is to say that, should we hold it up to empirical scrutiny, we will find that it is true of the world. We realize this as soon as we shift our attention from descriptions of, say, Sherlock Holmes (an annoyingly common example in the debate) and consider, for example, the disquisition on the nature of poverty in George Orwell's *Down and out in Paris and London*, the descriptions of New York's labyrinthine cityscapes in E. L. Doctorow's *City of God*, the bombing of Dresden in Kurt Vonnegut's *Slaughterhouse 5*, Napoleon's invasion of Russia in Leo Tolstoy's *War and Peace*, and the notoriously tedious accounts of whaling practices in Herman Melville's *Moby Dick*. Literary works borrow freely from our store of worldly facts in the construction of their fictional worlds, and so with a moment's reflection we realize that an extensive portion of literary content is not in any sense 'made-up', a construct of imaginative invention. This much the make-believe theorist will concede, of course. But the problem is graver than the make-believe theorist realizes.

I have argued throughout this book that we know to *read* these world-adequate descriptions as functioning to state 'facts' not about our world but about the world of the work of fiction. We suspend our interest in their truth for the sake of our participation in the narrative of literary work. The same basic insight is also common to the make-believe theory, and up to this point we are allies. But notice that on the make-believe theory a further step is taken, to the claim that we make-believe these sentences and descriptions *to be true*, that we *imagine* they are descriptive of something *real*. When we read works of narrative fiction, 'we are supposed to engage imaginatively with them, making-believe that the events narrated really have taken place, that the people described really do exist, and so on'. [25]

The trouble is that we are being asked to include world-adequate content under the scope of 'it is make-believe that'. This is a *very* strong claim, and we should not overlook how much it demands

---

[25] Friend, in Kieran and Lopes (2003: 37).

of us. The question at hand is whether it makes good sense, or *any* sense, to say that we make-believe material occurring in a work of fiction that we know to be empirically adequate or true-of-the world. If the answer is No, as I think it is, given the fact that literary content is often world-adequate, the make-believe theory turns out to be an implausible account of our imaginative encounters with literary works.

A simple point suffices to make clear just how much the make-believe theorist asks of us. If I say that I am making-believe a certain proposition, it implies that I do *not* believe the truth of the proposition; in other words, it implies that I will assent to the claim that it is *false*. This seems obvious. If I tell you that I am pretending that I am writing a chapter right now, the implication would be that I am not (really) writing a chapter right now. And, if you see that in fact I am writing my chapter when I tell you this, you would think something is wrong with my mental state, that at the very least I am deluded about whether I am, or am merely pretending that I am, writing my chapter. The reason for this is that the proposition 'I am making-believe that I am writing my chapter' implies the falsity of the proposition that 'I am (really) writing my chapter'.

In the same vein, when I read the swell of descriptions in a literary work that I know to be world-adequate, what gives any credibility to the idea that I make-believe them *to be true*, that, when I find sentences of this sort, I 'imagine or make-believe (but do not believe)'[26] them? In what sense do I not believe them? I do not believe that a literary work uses these descriptions to make truth claims about the world; I do not read them as asserted *by* the text *of* reality. But it is another, and altogether stronger, thing to say that I *make-believe* them. In the first case, there is no implication that I am committed to the falsity of the description. In the second case, as we are beginning to see, there is. Considering that works of literary fiction habitually construct aspects of its narrative upon a commonly known factual foundation, the make-believe theory invites the charge

---

[26] Lamarque and Olsen (1994: 34).

that it ends up building, if not outright contradiction, then a quite palpable tension into the basic attitude it claims we bring to a work of literary fiction.

Christopher New, whose criticism of the make-believe theory I am following here, puts it well when he argues:

Competent speakers of English would judge 'I am pretending' (or make-believe or non-deceptively pretending to myself) that I am famous, and 'I also believe that I am famous' as absurd as they would find the sentence 'I intend to pay the bill and I also believe that I have paid the bill' absurd. They would find it absurd for the same reasons they would find the sentence 'I assert that it is raining, yet I don't believe that it is raining' absurd: in each case, the speaker denies in the second part of his assertion that a condition for the truth of the first part—that he is pretending (make-believe), intends or asserts—has been fulfilled. True, it may be possible for someone both to assert that p and also not believe that p. But then he will believe that p and not believe that p; that is, he will have inconsistent beliefs.[27]

In this respect the make-believe theory just reintroduces, in inverted form, the traditional problem of fiction and belief. The standard problem is that, if we regard literature as trying to produce in us true beliefs about our world, we shall inevitably end up knocking up against its fictionality. Likewise, in introducing the concept of make-believe, we end up knocking up against those portions of literary content we know to have a factual basis or to be otherwise world-adequate.

The attitude the theory asks us to take towards literary content of this nature is a breach of an argument, christened Moore's Paradox, that has the status of a golden rule in logic and epistemology: it is unintelligible to describe one as believing what one knows to be false. For the same reason, we cannot make sense of the idea of making-believe what one knows to be true. Since literary content is teeming with truths—unasserted truths, but truths nonetheless—of all sorts, this turns out to be a very serious problem for the make-believe theorist.

[27] New (1996: 160).

Defenders of the make-believe theory often construct examples to show that we can in fact make-believe what we know to be true.[28] The proffered cases often have the following form. Imagine, say, a politician who, in the privacy of his study, looks in the mirror and makes-believe that he is addressing Parliament. Thus it is both true that he is a politician and that he makes-believe that he is a politician, and so one can, if the example is solid, pretend to be true what one knows to be true.

But this will not work. To get the required parallel with our experience of works of literary fiction, the example would have to show that *the same psychological state* can take its object both to be true (the proposition 'I am addressing Parliament') and to be make-believedly true. This is what it amounts to when applied to the act of reading works of literary fiction: that one and the same appreciative state can take its object to be true yet make-believe that it is true (for example, the various political and social events—all very much a part of Italian history and known to be such by the educated reader—that form the backdrop of Guiseppe di Lampedusa's *The Leopard*). For the example to yield this, one would have to imagine the politician engaged in this game of make-believe, not during his 'off hours', in the privacy of his own home, addressing an *imagined* audience. One would have to imagine him playing this game of make-believe while he is *actually* addressing Parliament—that is, when he is engaged in the very activity he is also making-believe himself to be engaged in. At this point, his behaviour appears to verge on the delusional.

In fact, the politician cannot *really* believe what he also makes-believe, for he does not, presumably, believe that he is also

---

[28] Walton's own example concerns a certain Fred, a shoe salesman who has daydreams in which he is wealthy and the object of affection, neither of which is true in the real world. But in these daydreams he 'imagines that his name is Fred, that he prefers warm climates, that Paris is in France, and much else that he knows to be true' (Walton 1990: 13). It is interesting, though perhaps just slightly, that when Walton develops this example he uses the weaker term 'imagine' instead of 'make-believe': he speaks of Fred imagining what he also knows to be true rather than casting it in terms of Fred making-believe to be true what he also knows to be true.

addressing Parliament when playing this game of make-believe. He knows himself to be in his study, preparing for his political duties, but not actually engaged in these duties. True, he is imagining himself to be a politician, and he also happens to be one. But he is not, in these private moments, *being* a politician; he is preparing for his tasks, perhaps; but he is not actually executing them. Thus examples of this sort will not help us understand how we can believe what we also make-believe in the required sense.

What the make-believe theorists have right is that we do not take the various world-adequate sentences we find in a literary work to be asserted of the world, as though a novel interrupts its construction of a fictional world at these points and suddenly, inexplicably, begins to make reports on how things stand in the world. This is surely right. But, if we take the extra step, as the make-believe theorist does, of asking that we *make*-believe these sentences *to be true*, we build into literary experience a quite nasty clashing with what we do in fact believe about the world. It turns our appreciation of literature into a place where our normal beliefs about the world become troublesome guests, and it is unclear why a theory of the imagination needs this extra step.

We have to ask ourselves what would make the theory attractive at this point, why we should want to add to the standard and reasonable claim that we understand literature to have the luxury of speaking in independence of truth and reality the claim that we make-believe what it says *to be true*. In the first case we push aside the relevance of truth and belief when we appreciate literary content. In the second case we reintroduce it, only now in the form of *fictional* truths that we *make*-believe, and in so doing we find ourselves saddled with new and unnecessary burdens. We do want to capture the independence of literary appreciation from questions of truth and belief. But we do not want to do this in such a way that we turn this independence into an antagonism, that we end up creating a friction between our worldly beliefs and our engagement with the content of a novel. An adequate theory of the imagination will give us *independence without conflict*, and the make-believe theory, at least in its canonical form, fails to provide this.[29]

The argument I have given concerns a small hole in the logic of the make-believe theory, and every position has its holes. But it is much more than a mere logical or semantic quibble. For this hole functions to reveal a considerable gap between the make-believe theory and our general intuitions about how we relate to works of literary fiction. The step from the sensible point that we do not take world-adequate sentences in literary worlds to be asserted of the world to the claim that we make-believe them to be true of the world just looks unnecessary and excessive after we have given this argument. As far as I can see, there is no remaining reason to accept the canonical version of the make-believe theory, particularly given the availability of a great number of less demanding and more intuitive theories of the imagination. Indeed, this is the most common criticism we find made of the make-believe theory—that it is just so intuitively unlikely that we are doing all that the make-believe theorist claims we are when reading fiction. As Noël Carroll argues:

I do not wish to deny that the consumers of novels, pictures, films and the like are active, but I am not convinced that they are involved in all of the role-playing Walton adduces. For example, when I read *Gone with the Wind*, I understand its propositions, but am I also additionally involved in a game of make-believe in which fictionally I know that Rhett Butler is

---

[29] At this point it is common to ask whether Walton (or make-believe theorists in general) offers an intuitive or acceptable account of what a game of make-believe is. For the reasons I have given against the idea that we can assume such a comprehensive attitude of 'it is fictionally true that' or 'it is make-believe that' to literature, one can ask whether it makes sense to claim that a child takes this sort of comprehensive, sweeping attitude of fictionality towards all of the bits of reality that are assumed or explicitly used in her game of make-believe: is this cup of tea still tea, or is it fictionally true that it is a cup of tea; of those very real friends she invites into the game does it become 'make-believedly' true that they are her friends, etc. (These examples are not mine. Thanks are due to someone for them, though I cannot recall whom.) In short, it seems unreasonable to attribute so much making-believe, so much pretending, even to a child's game of make-believe. I do not want to go into an examination of what we call games of make-believe, since it would take me too far off course. But this would be an obvious critical strategy.

dashing and debonair and Scarlett O'Hara is devious and determined... For example, we might think of fictions as invitations to entertain or suppose certain propositions as unasserted—supposing them without commitment. Fictions invite this stance. When I read a fiction it is not the case that I fictionally know Silas was a miser; rather, as I read, I entertain (as unasserted) the proposition that Silas was a miser.[30]

Anders Pettersson is also worth mentioning here:

> My conviction that Currie and Walton's analyses are incorrect is due mainly to the fact that I myself, as far as I know, never play games of make-believe when reading literature. As I read the *Old Man and the Sea*, I follow the unrolling of events, well aware that these are fictitious, and I react to what I read. I have what is sometimes solemnly called a literary experience. But I do not seem to enter a world of a game of make-believe, where I read an authentic account of the old man or listen to a veracious report about his actions (to do so to me seems entirely uncalled for: my feeling is that it would mix my literary experience with aesthetically irrelevant fantasies)... There are thus experienced fiction readers who deny, explicitly, that they use literature in the way Walton and Currie's theories postulate. This is clearly embarrassing for the theory.[31]

A moral can be found in the difficulties of the make-believe theory. We see a trap that we must avoid—namely, the temptation to allow our reflections on *fictions* to determine our theory of *literary* fiction. The tradition that leads to the make-believe theory begins with examples of sentences that describe patently 'made-up' objects or states of affairs—hence the reliance on examples of fictional detectives, imaginary heroines approaching death, and sundry monsters and creatures of the night. But to call a text a work of literary fiction is not thereby to claim that it is *from beginning to end* a continuous string of sentences all of which are fictional in the sense of being 'made up'. Literary texts are saturated with descriptions of every sort—psychological, historical, geographical, sexual, cultural, and so on—that are world-adequate, or at least cannot be modelled on the made-up. We should not want to model our understanding of

[30] Carroll (1995: 98–9).   [31] Pettersson (1993: 89).

a work of literary fiction on our understanding of obviously fictional sentence, for a viable theory of the latter—which the make-believe theory arguably does provide—will not give us a plausible account of the former. No one would deny this, and I do not want to be taken as suggesting that any make-believe theorist actually does. But the make-believe theorist does appear to fail to take it *seriously*, to see how at odds with this fact the theory is.

Walton, with his characteristic wit, claimed that John Searle suffered from the 'Have Theory, Will Travel' syndrome when he tried to import his speech-act theory to the study of literary fiction.[32] One would not be too far off the mark to bring the same charge against the popularity in analytical aesthetics of applying a theory of make-believe, tailored for explaining our understanding of obviously fictional characters and events, to models of the imaginative structure of *literary-textual* appreciation. The make-believe theory might explain why I cower when I see a menacing slime on a cinema screen, as Walton convincingly argues. But it is too much to think that it accounts for the basic nature of our imaginative engagement with the whole of a literary work of art.

The larger motivation for my reluctance to accept the make-believe theory is that it seems ill suited for a substantial account of literary humanism. It looks to be ultimately a return to the picture of fiction as fodder for fantasy, and this picture has never been helpful to humanists. There is no clear way to understand how we could use the vocabulary of make-believe to account for the idea that we can *see* reality in the fictional worlds of literary texts. The call to identify our appreciation of a literary work with a game of make-believe amounts to cutting ourselves off from the directness of literature's presentation of reality that I have argued is central to a viable model of humanism. The attitude of make-believe builds into the fictive stance an antagonism with reality. And it does this, ironically, in its attempt to bring literature closer to reality. If we argue that we read fiction *as though it were real*, making-believe that we are

[32] Walton (1990: 76).

viewing actual people and events, we do, as the make-believe theorists argue, give our engagement with a work of fiction the vividness, the semblance, of our-worldly experience. But the price we pay for this is that we make impossible the move from the idea that we pretend to see our world in fiction to the claim that we actually do see it, for the make-believe operator brings too much in our field of appreciation under its scope. As such, we will not be able to do justice to the critical and cognitive force of literature. We end trapping ourselves in a game of make-believe rather than allowing literature, at least when it wishes, to open up on to reality.

5.3. A CASE FOR OPENNESS

Neither panfictionalism nor the make-believe theory poses a real challenge to the literary humanist. Contrary to a common fear, panfictionalism does not give us reason to think that the humanist cannot speak of literary works as directing us towards reality, for on inspection we saw that panfictionalism offers no reasons to deny that we can read texts, literary or otherwise, as directing us towards our world, regardless of how we give metaphysical sense to the notion of 'the world'. And, since the make-believe theory does not hold up under scrutiny, we need not worry that the humanist ought to replace talk of seeing reality in literature with talk of making-believe that we see reality.

But something of broader importance comes out of these discussions. Both panfictionalism and the make-believe theory put on display, though again in very different ways, a common tendency in literary aesthetics. It is the tendency to pull apart two stances that we must reconcile if we are to do justice to literary humanism, indeed if we are to have anything intelligent or convincing to say when we speak about the relationship between literature and life. The stances are what I earlier called the fictive and the worldly stance—that is, the stance we assume towards content we take to be the product of imaginative creation and the stance we take towards content we take to be attempting to cast light on reality. Literary humanism, if it is to be worth its salt as a theory about how we experience works of literature, must give sense to the idea that the frame of fiction can also offer a window on the world: it must show that these two stances can work in tandem. Indeed, humanism, if understood as designating a way of confronting works of art, *is* just the claim that we can regard a work of literature as opening up on to reality while also, and at the same time, explicitly presenting its content as fictional.

This is what so few theories of fiction currently in philosophical circulation allow, if not intentionally then certainly by implication. What we find in most popular theories of fiction is a parsing apart of the worldly and the fictional to such an extent that reality is effectively banished (one imagines Baudrillard very pleased). We see this quite clearly in the make-believe theory, giving us as it does make-believedly 'real' objects but never the real thing itself. In the case of panfictionalism, it is taken as granted that literature brings fictions and only fictions to view. But, instead of accepting this and admitting that literature is therefore just a game of fantasy, panfictionalists feel a sting, realizing that this invites the prejudice that texts subsumed under the fictive stance are to be contrasted unfavourably with 'serious' texts that call for a worldly stance and so an appreciation of reality. To take the sting out of this, panfictionalists set themselves the goal of showing that there is really no stance other than the fictive stance, at least for the savvy reader who has been disabused of that quaint belief in reality. For both panfictionalists and make-believe theorists, the implicit assumption seems to be that, since a work of literature presents fictions to view, the stance we takes toward it 'ex hypothesi' cannot be open to 'a view of the real world'.[33] The task for them then becomes to show either that literature offers make-believe worlds or that all we have in any case are fictional worlds—but in neither case the real world. Whence this antagonism between the fictional and the real?

---

[33] Lamarque (1996: 105). The full passage was quoted at the beginning of Chapter 4.

What literary aesthetics desperately needs is to find a way of talking about works of imaginative literature that can acknowledge both, and in the same breath, the fictionality and the worldliness of literary content. That is, it must devise theories of fiction that can accommodate *each* stance, not as an occasional occurrence, but as a unified stance that marks one of the basic modes of encountering literary works. What literary aesthetics presently has at its disposal is a vocabulary that in effect accounts only for the fictive stance, leaving us without a theoretically respectable word to say about the presence of the real in the literary work of art. It is a decidedly one-sided approach to literature, top heavy with impressive accounts of the fictional yet accounts virtually all of which make it impossible to speak sensibly about the 'real' dimension of literature. Again, I doubt this is quite intentional, though panfictionalists do seem quite happy with it. But it is nonetheless the consequence of how philosophers, on both sides of the analytic/continental divide, tell us how to speak about the fictions we find in literature.

It is very odd that we should have built such an antagonism into our theories of fiction. For, if we look outside literature, it is rather easy to find cultural practices that use fictions as a medium for exploring the real. In fact, it seems to be only when we consider literature that we speak about fictions as somehow constitutionally opposed to the real. If we switch perspectives, leaving aside for a moment the arts, it becomes clear that we have a general idea that the fictional and the real come together quite easily, and quite frequently.

Consider, for a moment, thought experiments. In its broadest sense, a thought experiment is a particular employment of hypothetical reasoning. It is an investigation of reality that begins by asking 'what if " ... "' or 'imagine that " ... "' and proceeds to describe an invented scenario.[34] A thought experiment is, in this sense, the familiar practice of positing a scenario and asking how, given the particular way it teases and confronts some intuition or concept, it reflects back on the world and tells us something about our culture

---

[34] See Rescher, in Horowitz and Massey (1991).

(or our scientific theories, our language, a moral theory, and so on). The common examples are well known. From the hard sciences we have the case of Schrödinger's cat to refute the Copenhagen theory of quantum physics. In philosophy we have examples such as Socrates' conversation with the Laws of Athens, Descartes's Evil Genius, Wittgenstein's so-called beetle box argument, and Nagel's wondering what it would be like to be a bat.

The following is a standard statement of the nature of a thought experiment:

A 'thought experiment' is an attempt to draw instruction from a process of hypothetical reasoning that proceeds by eliciting the consequence of an hypothesis which, for aught that one actually knows to the contrary, may well be false. It consists in reasoning from a supposition that is not accepted as true—perhaps even known to be false—but is assumed provisionally in the interest of making a point or resolving a conclusion.[35]

In other words, thought experiments and literary fictions have at least this much in common: our attitude towards the scenarios described is that of the fictive stance. The claim that the hypothetical scenarios of thought experiments are 'assumed' even when 'known to be false' is philosopher-sprecht for what in less lofty conversations we refer to as fictions.

Now there are obviously many qualities that literature and thought experiments do *not* have in common. Most noticeable among them is the fact that thought experiments do, and works of literary fiction do not, situate their fictions in a larger 'process of hypothetical reasoning'.[36] This would seem a rather crucial difference, and enough to make one suspicious of the occasional attempt to treat literary works

---

[35] See Rescher, in Horowitz and Massey 31.

[36] I hope this makes it clear that here I am not arguing for the claim that literary works can function as thought experiments, or that the parallel between the two that I draw here gives us a way of understanding how literature might possess cognitive value. Besides my brief comment here, the arguments of Chapters 1 and 3 should make it clear that I would not endorse such an approach to a defence of humanism. I thank a referee for OUP for bringing to my attention that an earlier draft of this chapter suggested otherwise.

as a species of philosophical thought experiment.[37] But they do share the use of fictions. If it is true, as it is often put, that the basic condition of the fictive stances is that it calls on the reader to treat a described scenario as 'beyond truth-valuation',[38] that it assumes that 'how things are is determined by how they are described in the text'[39] (and not by world relations), a scenario in a thought experiment has at least the call to take the fictive stance towards its contents in common with literature.

Now what does the parallel tell us? If thought experiments can be seen as utilizing the basic ingredient of the fictive stance, we have a model that reveals a basic compatibility between the worldly and the fictive stance—as simple as the parallel is, it effectively drains us of any feeling of antagonism. For, when reading a thought experiment, we are asked (however we precisely want to explain this, and it will probably differ from example to example) to see the fictions presented as localizing a set of 'real' interests. We read Putnam's 'brain in the vat' as calling into question various conceptions of human identity, Socrates' conversation with the Athenian Laws is read as also speaking about *our*—or at least the Athenians'—laws. It is built into our concept of a thought experiment that it functions to instruct us about our world (we might recall here Wittgenstein's claim that 'nothing is more important for teaching us to understand the concepts we have than constructing fictitious ones'[40]). In short, what we get from the thought-experiment parallel is what we might

---

[37] Noël Carroll (2002) and Catherine Elgin (in Gibson, Huemer, and Pocci 2007) have offered what I think are the most compelling arguments for the assimilation of (at least some) works of literary fiction to thought experiments. Though I am not partial to this line of argument (see the above footnote), their arguments are very impressive. An approach I do find convincing is Eileen John's treatment of what literary fiction has in common with thought experiments, one that recognizes that the point of commonality does not entitle us to treat works of fiction as a variety of thought experiment: 'We can thus think of some works of fiction as functioning like philosophers' thought experiments, in which problematic imagined cases are used to prompt responses relevant to philosophical problems and address questions about our conceptual scheme' (John 1998: 321). I take the 'like' to be crucial, and to stop somewhat short of a full identification of literature with a thought experiment.

[38] Doležel (1998: 5).   [39] Lamarque and Olsen (1994: 99).
[40] Wittgenstein (1980: 74e).

call a model of *openness*, an example that gives the air of intuitiveness to the claim that we can, and do, think it is possible that the frame of fiction can offer a window on the world.

If this is so, we can see that something is probably amiss when philosophers argue that 'both fictive utterances and fictive reports create a gap between the content described and the actual world. The gap is primarily inferential; in presenting a story, or reporting on it, a speaker blocks inferences from fictional content to how things are in the world.'[41] Indeed a gap is created, but only of the dull and obvious sort. Just as we do not fear the end of the world when we read *War of the Worlds*, we never cower when we read descriptions of Nozick's Utility Monster or Descartes's Evil Genius. Questions of existence do not enter into our appreciation of fictions, and so there is a conceptual gap between the description of a fiction and the idea of its actuality. Fictions are explicitly presented so that their descriptions can be entertained rather than brought under the categories of truth and reference. Nevertheless, this does not mean that we are not working through reality when working our way through textual content presented under the fictive stance, and the thought experiment parallel forces us to come to terms with this. The general idea we find in writings on literary fiction that the fictive stance necessarily excludes (or at least is by nature a turning-away from) a worldly stance is not sustainable after we point out that it is done as a matter of daily endeavour in intellectual activities as common as philosophy and science.

I would like to switch gears and look at a very different practice, much more playful than thought experiments but just as interesting for our purposes: the musical lyric. We might think, if we are not circumspect, that we have three and only three choices whenever we run into a proper name or personal pronoun: we can say that it refers to or stands for an *actual* particular, a *fictional* particular, or, failing to designate either, *nothing*. This sounds reasonable, but it misses another possibility. Try, if you believe that these are the only

---

[41] Lamarque and Olsen (1994: 88).

The Fictional and the Real 179

choices, to make sense of the refrain from Cole Porter's 'Anything Goes':

> If old hymns you like
> If bare limbs you like
> If Mae West you like
> Or me undressed you like
> why nobody will oppose
> —anything goes

Who is this 'you' Cole Porter is singing about? If we think that it is a fictional particular, we will run in great trouble. No proper *story* is told in this song, and thus there is nothing to give domicile to a genuinely fictional character: as real people live in real worlds, so fictional characters live in fictional worlds. If this 'you' does not designate a proper fictional particular, then perhaps we should look for an actual particular, say *you*, the listener—singers, after all, do sing to their audiences. Though you are closer to the right answer, no strict sense can be made of this. If we really thought the 'you' picked out *you* the listener, we will run into the incontrovertible fact that Porter, long deceased, certainly could not have had *you* in mind when he wrote or sang the song. And it cannot be right, can it, to say that the song is about no one, nothing?

Take another example, the chorus from 'Lush Life'.

> I'll forget you
> I will
> Yet you are still burning inside my brain
> Romance is mush
> stifling those who strive
> I'll live a lush life in some small dive
> And there I'll be
> While I rot with the rest
> Of those whose lives are lonely, too

Now who is this 'I'? When Billy Strayhorn wrote this song, he may very well have had someone in mind, perhaps himself (surely songs can be autobiographical). But when Billie Holiday sings 'Lush Life' I doubt she too is singing about Billy Strayhorn: her 'I' is not his 'I'. Perhaps the 'I' designates each singer of the song, switching residence with each person who offers his or her voice to it. But this cannot be, unless we think singers are describing themselves when they perform. And that they do not is brought home as soon as Billie Holiday, quite female, goes on to sing 'I'm Just a Gigolo'.

Let us look at one more song, a few lines from the old Edith Piaf standard 'La Vie en rose' (in English of course).

> And when you speak
> angels sing from above
> and everyday words turn into love songs
> give your heart and soul to me
> and life will always be
> la vie en rose

One wonderful thing about shamelessly romantic songs is that we know so well how to listen to them. There really is no challenge in identifying who the 'you' is if we ask this as a cultural question rather than as a theoretical puzzle. We know, if we know anything at all about how to listen to music, that songs of these sorts are about everyone and yet no one at all, neither an actual nor a fictional character but then still not no one. That is to say, we do not take them to be about merely *particular* lovers.

No argument is needed for this, for a few platitudes will suffice. These songs are about *every* lover while speaking of no *one* lover. The 'I' of 'Lush Life' is the 'I' of the dejected lover: it is *his* song. The 'you' in 'La Vie en rose' is the object of intoxicating love: this song is sung to *her*. There is nothing mysterious in this, as though we think that we now need to go on to investigate entities of some strange sort, say The Dejected Lover as Such. The songs have the role of describing *characters of culture*, 'I-s' and 'you-s' that draw together and hold in place features of shared human experience. We might say, with a risk of sounding purple, that the I of 'Lush Life' is the voice of 'our form of life', that 'La Vie en rose' is the crooning of what our culture calls the moment of enthralment.

Now, if we turn these nebulous pronouns into genuine fictional particulars, giving them a name and a genuine narrative context, there is no reason to think that they will lose their ability to reflect our culture, that once we begin to treat them as fictions we shall somehow have to ignore their ability to frame aspects of general experience. When Rodolfo sings 'O suave fanciulla' to Mimì, what would make us think that he cannot do, just because he lives in the fictional world of *La Bohème*, what the 'you' in 'Anything Goes' or 'La Vie en rose' does—that Puccini, in all his effort, could not accomplish what Cole Porter did with a much simpler song? And, if it seems reasonable to step from Porter to Puccini, what plausible reason would we have for thinking that the step cannot be made from Puccini to Shakespeare, from Rodolfo and Mimì to Romeo and Juliet: from words that are sung to words that are written or spoken on a theatre stage?

What these reflections remind us of—something we probably already knew, though we might forget it when reading philosophical theories of fiction—is that we have a general understanding that fictions can, and are regularly employed to, embody various regions of human experience.[42] And we understand them to be able to reflect back to us what we put into them, this culture of which both they and we are a part.

This does not introduce a tension between the particularity of the fiction and the aspects of cultural life we take these characters to localize, for there is no obvious antagonism between the cultural and the 'un-real' aspects of a fiction. The fiction acts as a kind of linchpin. It holds together a particular view of our world. But—we want to

---

[42] As Jonathan Culler says, 'Fiction can hold together within a single space a variety of languages, levels of focus, points of view' (Culler 1975: 261).

say—it is the particular, the fictional character, who is holding it together, essential rather than sacrificed in this act of opening our culture up to view. And it is part of understanding what fictions are to treat them as such—to respect, we might say, that it is Rodolfo, or Romeo, we are appreciating, but to allow ourselves to be open to what these characters have to show us. In short, far from there being a conceptual rift between the fictive and the worldly, their rapport is part of our idea of ways of using, and reading, fictions.

What fictions are especially well suited for doing, precisely because they are fictions, is to hold in place something general, something *katholou*, as Aristotle would have it. By directing our attention away from the merely, or purely, particular, they are able to weave together a view of what Richard Eldridge calls 'the complex texture of our human lives'.[43] This is something our own individual lives might also bring to view, in their own little ways. But it is surely something we rarely put on display as well as our great literary characters do. At any rate, we certainly are not *read* as Othello, Emma, or Bartleby are—unless perhaps on a psychiatrist's couch—and thus we do not offer the same occasion for shared, public revelation as the great characters of fiction.[44]

This does not in any way suggest that we should not regard fictions as just that, as though calling for this openness requires treating, say, Iago as something other than an imaginary character. What it does ask us to deny is the appropriateness of a *merely* fictional stance towards literary content; it asks that we do not read works of fiction as a sort of imaginative reduplication of empirical discourse, a place where we just find 'facts' stated about made-up people and events.

---

[43] Eldridge (2003a: 226).
[44] An excellent statement of this idea, one that I am indebted to here, is Bernard Harrison's claim that in Virginia Woolf's *To the Lighthouse* we find that 'the textuality which constitutes Mr Ramsey's personality is, then, not a textuality of words alone, but a textuality of practices. And since we share those practices, and are also in part constituted as individuals by them, the practices out of which Mr Ramsey is constructed link him not merely to the reality of the world present to all of us as the condition of our speaking a common language, but to the reality which we constitute: to us, as readers' (Harrison, in Gibson and Huemer 2004: 105).

The fear, I would think, is that in calling on this openness of appreciation we might fall into an old trap, that of crushing the fictive stance under the weight of the worldly stance. Certainly some forms of humanism fall into this trap—namely, mimetic varieties: that is, any version of humanism that claims that the connection between literature and life is fundamentally a matter of fiction 'mirroring' the real world. Once we say this, and then go on to claim that in appreciation we are ultimately directed towards that of which they are representations (some actual state of affairs, the real prototype of which the fiction is a symbol, and so on.), we do sacrifice the fictive stance, allowing room, in effect, only for an appreciation of the real. This is violence to the idea of the literary, and a very cheap route to humanism, one that ultimately tries to make literature relevant to the our-worldly by denying that there is really any fiction in literature. We do not want to cancel out the fictive stance in calling on this openness to the real. We avoid this mistake by giving up the notion that the connection to external reality comes in the form of a mimetic duplication of the actual world.

Rather, we argue that, in the construction of their worlds, works of literary fiction can bring the structure of ours into view: that the connection lies in the shared fabric out of which both our cultural reality and fictional worlds are woven. The worldly stance does not call on us to try, impossibly and foolishly, to deny Othello's fictionality and try to turn him into a mirror image of our world (say the Jealous Man). He represents nothing real. But we see in him our standards of representation, our criteria, our sense-bestowing linguistic and social practices, practices that are found in any world that is intelligible to us (it is at times important to remind ourselves how much is implied by the simple fact that fiction is intelligible to us). To bring literature under the fictive stance is to allow the worlds it describes to be free from the actual world. To add to this the worldly stance is to allow these thoroughly fictional worlds to bring to view what they take from us in their creation. In short, to be humanists we do not need to take a fictional world in any way to be a picture of our world. We need only to claim that *in* fictions we can see this shared stage, this undercurrent of common reality, indeed often, as Dostoevsky tells us, 'more clearly than is usually shown'. This, at any rate, is what I hope to have shown in this book.

Conclusion

I trust that I have summed up my argument for literary humanism frequently enough in the past chapters that I need not do so again here. So, in conclusion, let me just offer a brief word about what I have tried to accomplish here.

Perhaps the most significant feature of the approach to humanism I have recommended is that it shows us that we need not fear that we will lose touch with the literary if we embrace the humanist intuition. The distrust many have of literary humanism is that it often seems that becoming humanists is tantamount to renouncing our promise to say something informative of the nature of literature. This came out clearly in the criticisms I offered of the indirect and truth-seeking approaches to humanism, forms of humanism that bring to light the ease with which the humanist can let the literary work slip away in the attempt to unite it with reality. The theory of humanism I have offered in this book shows us that we can be both humanists and faithful literary theorists. It reveals the connection between literature and life to be a proper feature of literary content. And, if this is so, it gives us a way of seeing how a reasonably developed theory of humanism can cast light on rather than turn us away from the nature of literary experience.

In making a case for this, I also hope to have shown that we can part entirely from the traditional humanistic strategy for making the passage from literature to life—namely, that of relying on a mimetic theory of literary fiction. The urge to invent a theory of mimesis for translating fictions into actualities is great for the humanist, and anyone who has been drawn to a defence of humanism has at one time or other felt its pull. If we try to turn fictions into reflections of actuality, there is no trouble in making literature relevant to our world, for, as soon as we open a novel, we find that we are already there—indeed we find that literature never offers an occasion to leave this world. But, as I have argued, this is also the most unreasonable route to humanism. As one literary theorist puts it:

> Mimetic doctrine is behind a very popular mode of reading that converts fictional persons into live people, imaginary settings into actual places, invented stories into real-life happenings. Mimetic reading, practiced by naive readers and reinforced by journalistic critics, is one of the most reductive operations of which the human mind is capable: the vast, open, and inviting universe of fictional discourse is shrunk to the model of one single world, actual human experience.[1]

Much of the value of the sceptic in this book was to force the humanist to avoid this single-world model of fiction. In taking the sceptic seriously, I hope to have shown that it is possible to defend a theory of humanism that can without qualification accept that literature trades in the construction of fictional worlds rather than in the building of mirrors held up to the actual world. We saw, in short, that we can maintain a connection between literature and reality without resting humanism on a foundation of the traditional representationalist view of literature. As such, humanism turns out to be compatible even with 'strong' theories of fictional discourse and it thus can sit well with and be of use to the great number of theories of literature that take as their starting point a rejection of representational and mimetic models of fiction.

The world-wise philosopher might cringe at my dismissal in this book of talk not only of representation but also, and perhaps more importantly, of truth and knowledge when describing how literary works relate to reality. One might well think that with a bit of tinkering one can redefine these terms a bit and find perfectly legitimate ways to reintegrate them in a model of humanism. I

---

[1] Doležel (1998: p. iv).

should confess that I also think that this is possible. What I hope to have shown, ultimately, is not so much that these terms are beyond repair and ought to be thrown aside. It is rather that a viable theory of humanism is, contrary to a long-standing prejudice, not dependent on them at all. The debate between sceptics and humanists is often thought to hinge on whether literature can represent reality, state truths about it, and otherwise yield knowledge of the world. What is important is not whether these terms have any literary application. It is to see that one can be a humanist without them, and thus that the debate need not spin around these terms exclusively, as it very often does. And, if we can find a way to be humanists with these terms, we have a chance of actually moving the debate ahead and, hopefully, into new territory.

Perhaps this is a case where a plea might be strengthened by weakening it. I would like to think that I have made the theory of humanism offered in this book both plausible and attractive. But, if I have failed to convince one of this, it would be just as satisfying to have made it appear reasonable to want to be humanists at all. Even if one is not sold on the precise shape in which I am selling humanism, I would be content if I have given the reader a sense of how interesting and important it is to ask the questions raised here, and that both philosophy and literary theory can benefit from it.

References

ARISTOTLE (1987). *Poetics*, trans. Richard Janko. Indianapolis: Hackett.
ATTRIDGE, DEREK (2004). *The Singularity of Literature*. London: Routledge.
BARRETT, CYRIL (ed.) (1965). *Collected Papers on Aesthetics*. Oxford. Blackwell.
BARTHES, ROLAND (1974). *S/Z: An Essay*, trans. Richard Miller. New York: Hill & Wang.
—— (1977). *Image–Music–Text*. New York: Hill and Wang.
BATES, STANLEY (1998). 'Review of Peter Lamarque's *Fictional Points of View*', *Philosophical Books*, 39/1: 78–81.
BAUDRILLARD, JEAN (1983*a*). *In the Shadow of the Silent Majorities, or, the End of the Social and Other Essays*. New York: Semiotext(e).
—— (1983*b*). *Simulations*. New York: Simiotext(e).
BEARDSLEY, MONROE (1970). 'The Aesthetic Point of View', *Metaphilosophy*, 1: 39–58.
—— (1978). 'Aesthetic Intentions and Fictive Illocutions', in *What Is Literature?*, ed. P. Hernadi. Bloomington, IN: Indiana University Press.
—— (1981). *Aesthetics: Problems in the Philosophy of Criticism*. Indianapolis: Hackett.
BEARDSMORE, R. W. (1971). *Art and Morality*. London: McMillan.
BELSEY, CATHERINE (2002). *Poststructuralism: A Very Short Introduction*. Oxford: Oxford University Press.
BENTHAM, JEREMY (1951). *Bentham's Theory of Fictions*, ed. C. K. Olden. London: Routledge.
BERTENS, HANS (1995). *The Idea of the Postmodern: A History*. London: Routledge.
BEST, STEVEN, AND KELLNER, DOUGLAS (1991). *Postmodern Theory: Critical Interrogations*. New York: Guilford Press.
BLACKBURN, SIMON (1998). 'Realism and Truth: Wittgenstein, Wright, Rorty and Minimalism', *Mind*, 107: 157–81.
BLOOM, HAROLD (1998). *Shakespeare: The Invention of the Human*. New York: Riverhead Books.
BOGHOSSIAN, PAUL (2006). *Fear of Knowledge: Against Relativism and Constructivism*. Oxford: Oxford University Press.

BOOTH, WAYNE (1961). *The Rhetoric of Fiction*. Chicago: University of Chicago Press.

BRANDOM, ROBERT B. (1994). *Making It Explicit*. Cambridge, MA: Harvard Univeristy Press.

BROOKS, CLEANTH (1968). *The Well Wrought Urn: Studies in the Structure of Poetry*. New York: Harcourt.

BURNS, GERALD L. (1999). *Tragic Thoughts at the End of Philosophy: Language, Literature, and Ethical Theory*. Evanston: Northwestern University Press.

CARROLL, NOËL (1988). 'Art, Practice, and Narrative', *The Monist*, 71: 140–56.

—— (1995). 'Kendall L Walton's *Mimesis as Make-Believe*', *Philosophical Quarterly*, 45: 93–9.

—— (2000). 'Art and Ethical Criticism: An Overview of Recent Directions of Research', *Ethics*, 110: 351–87.

—— (2002). 'The Wheel of Virtue: Art, Literature, and Moral Knowledge', *Journal of Aesthetics and Art Criticism*, 60: 3–26.

CAVELL, STANLEY (1969). *Must We Mean What We Say? A Book of Essays*. New York: Charles Scribner's Sons.

—— (1979). *The Claim of Reason: Wittgenstein, Skepticism, Morality, and Tragedy*. Oxford: Clarendon Press.

—— (1984). *Themes Out of School: Effects and Causes*. Chicago: University of Chicago Press.

—— (1987). *Disowning Knowledge: In Seven Plays of Shakespeare*. Cambridge: Cambridge University Press.

—— (1988). *In Quest of the Ordinary: Lines of Skepticism and Romanticism*. Chicago: University of Chicago Press.

CHARLTON, WILLIAM (1974). 'Is Philosophy a Kind of Literature?' *British Journal of Aesthetics*, 14: 3–16.

COLERIDGE, SAMUEL TAYLOR (1960). *Coleridge: Shakespeare Criticism*, I, ed. Thomas Midlleton Raysor. London: Everyman's Library.

COOPER, DAVID E. (2003). *Meaning*. Montreal: McGill-Queen's University Press.

CRITCHLEY, SIMON (2005). *Things Merely Are: Philosophy in the Poetry of Wallace Stevens*. New York: Routledge.

CULLER, JONATHAN (1975). *Structuralist Poetics: Structuralism, Linguistics and the Study of Literature*. London: Routledge.

CURRIE, GREGORY (1985). 'What is Fiction?' *Journal of Aesthetics and Art Criticism* 43: 385–92.
—— (1990). *The Nature of Fiction*. Cambridge: Cambridge University Press.
—— (1995). 'The Moral Psychology of Fiction', *Australasian Journal of Philosophy*, 73: 250–9.
DANTO, ARTHUR (1964). 'The Art World', *Journal of Philosophy*, 61: 571–84.
DAVENPORT, EDWARD (1983). 'Literature as Thought Experiment', *Philosophy of the Social Sciences*, 13: 279–306.
DAVIES, STEPHEN (2006). *Introduction to the Philosophy of Art*. Oxford: Blackwell.
DAVIS, TONY (1996). *Humanism*. London: Routledge.
DE BOLLA, PETER (2001). *Art Matters*. Cambridge, MA: Harvard University Press.
DE MAN, PAUL (1979). *Allegories of Fiction: Figural Language in Rousseau, Nietzsche, Rilke and Proust*. New Haven: Yale University Press.
DE SOUSA, RONALD (1987). *The Rationality of Emotion*. Cambridge, MA: MIT Press.
DELEUZE, GILLES, AND GUATTARI, FELÉX (1997). 'Literature and Life', trans. Daniel W. Smith and Michael A. Greco. *Critical Inquiry* 23: 225–30.
DERRIDA, JACQUES (1976). *On Grammatology*, trans. Gayatri Chakravorty. Baltimore: Johns Hopkins University Press.
—— (1977). 'Limited Inc.', *Glyph* 2: 162–254.
—— (1978). *Writing and Difference*, trans. Alan Bass. Chicago: University of Chicago Press.
DESCARTES, RENÉ (1991). *The Philosophical Writings of Descartes*, iii, ed. J. Cottingham, R. Stoothoff, D. Murdoch and A. Kenny. Cambridge: Cambridge University Press.
DIAMOND, CORA (1983–4). 'Having a Rough Story about What Moral Philosophy Is', *New Literary History,* 15: 155–70.
DICKENS, CHARLES (2003). *Oliver Twist*. New York: Penguin Classics.
DIFFEY, T. J. (1995). 'What Can We Learn from Art?' *Australasian Journal of Philosophy*, 73: 204–11.
DOLEŽEL, LUBOMÍR (1998). *Heterocosmica*. Baltimore: Johns Hopkins University Press, 1998.

DOSTOEVSKY, FYODOR (2001). *Notes from Underground*, in *The Best Short Stories of Fyodor Dostoevsky*, trans. David Magarshack. New York: Modern Library.

DUMMETT, MICHAEL (1973). *Frege: Philosophy of Language*. London: Duckworth.

―― (1978). *Truth and Other Enigmas*. Cambridge, MA: Harvard University Press.

EAGLETON, TERRY (1997). *Literary Theory: An Introduction*. 2nd edn. Oxford: Oxford University Press.

―― (2005). *The English Novel: An Introduction*. Oxford: Oxford University Press.

ECO, UMBERTO (1989). *The Open Work*. Cambridge, MA: Harvard University Press.

―― (1990). *The Limits of Interpretation*. Bloomington, IN: Indiana University Press.

―― (1994). *Interpretation and Overinterpretation*. Cambridge: Cambridge University Press.

ELDRIDGE, RICHARD (1989). *On Moral Personhood: Philosophy, Literature, Criticism, and Self-Understanding*. Chicago: University of Chicago Press.

―― (1997). *Leading a Human Life: Wittgenstein, Intentionality, and Romanticism*. Chicago: University of Chicago Press.

―― (2001). *The Persistence of Romanticism: Essays in Philosophy and Literature*. Cambridge: Cambridge University Press.

―― (2003*a*). *An Introduction to the Philosophy of Art*. Cambridge: Cambridge University Press.

―― (ed.) (2003*b*). *Stanley Cavell*. Cambridge: Cambridge University Press.

EVANS, GARETH (1982). *The Varieties of Reference*, ed. John McDowell. Oxford: Oxford University.

FARRELL, FRANK (2004). *Why Does Literature Matter*. Ithaca, NY: Cornell University Press.

FAULKNER, WILLIAM (1994). *The Sound and the Fury*. New York: W. W. Norton & Company.

FISCHER, MICHAEL (1989). *Stanley Cavell and Literary Skepticism*. Chicago: University of Chicago Press.

FISH, STANLEY (1980). Is *There a Text in this Class? The Authority of Interpretive Communities*. Cambridge, MA: Harvard University Press.

FREELAND, CYNTHIA (1997). 'Art and Moral Knowledge', *Philosophical Topics*, 25: 11–35.

FREGE, GOTTLIEB (1970). 'On Sense and Reference', in *Philosophical Writings of Gottlob Frege*, trans. and ed. Peter Geach and Max Black. Oxford: Oxford University Press.

GASKIN, RICHARD (1994). 'Symposium: Truth, Meaning and Literature', *British Journal of Aesthetics*, 34: 376–88.

GASS, WILLIAM (1996). *Finding a Form*. New York: Alfred A. Knopf.

GAUT, BERYS, AND LOPES, DOMINIC MCIVER (2001) (eds.), *The Routledge Companion to Aesthetics*. London: Routledge.

GIBSON, JOHN (2003). 'Between Truth and Triviality', *British Journal of Aesthetics*, 43: 224–37.

——— AND HUEMER, WOLFGANG (eds.) (2004). *The Literary Wittgenstein*. London: Routledge.

——— ——— AND POCCI, LUCA (2007). *A Sense of the World: Essays on Fiction, Narrative, and Knowledge*. London: Routledge.

GILL, CHRISTOPHER (1983). 'Did Chrysippus Understand *Media*', *Phronesis*, 28: 136–49.

GOODMAN, NELSON (1978). *Ways of Worldmaking*. Indianapolis: Hackett.

GRAHAM, GORDON (1995). 'Learning from Art', *British Journal of Aesthetics*, 35: 26–37.

GRICE, H. P. (1969). 'Utterer's Meaning and Intentions', *Philosophical Review*, 78: 147–77.

GUETTI, JAMES (1993). *Wittgenstein and the Grammar of Literary Experience*. Athens, GA: University of Georgia Press

HALLER, RUDOLF (1988). *Questions on Wittgenstein*, trans. Jane Braaten. London: Routledge.

HAMMER, ESPEN (2002). *Stanley Cavell: Skepticism, Subjectivity, and the Ordinary*. Cambridge: Polity Press.

HAROLD, JAMES (2003). 'Flexing the Imagination', *Journal of Aesthetics and Art Criticism*, 6: 247–58.

HARRISON, BERNARD (1991). *Inconvenient Fictions: Fiction and the Limits of Theory*. New Haven: Yale University Press.

HARTMAN, GEOFFREY (1981). *Saving the Text: Literature/Derrida/Philosophy*. Baltimore: Johns Hopkins University Press.

HERTZBERG, LARS (1976). 'On the Factual Dependence of the Language-Games', *Acta Philosophica Fennica*, 28: 126–53.

HIRSCH, E. D. (1976). *The Aims of Interpretation*. Chicago: University of Chicago Press.

HJORT, METTE, AND LAVER, SUE (eds.) (1997). *Emotion and the Arts*. New York: Oxford University Press.

HOROWITZ, TAMARA, AND MASSEY, G. J. (eds.) (1991). *Thought Experiments in Science and Philosophy*. Maryland: Rowman & Littlefield.

HUME, DAVID (1963). *Essays, Moral, Political and Literary*. Oxford: Oxford University Press.

—— (1975). *Enquiry Concerning Human Understanding*, ed. P. H. Nidditch. Oxford: Clarendon Press.

ISEMINGER, GARRY (1992) (ed.), *Intention and Interpretation*. Philadelphia: Temple University Press.

ISENBERG, ARNOLD (1954–5). 'The Problem of Belief', *Journal of Aesthetics and Art Criticism*, 13: 395–407.

ISER, WOLFGANG (1993). *The Fictive and the Imaginary: Charting Literary Anthropology*. Baltimore: Johns Hopkins University Press.

JAMES, WILLIAM (1971). *Selections*. New York: Harper & Row.

JOHN, EILEEN (1998). 'Reading Fiction and Conceptual Knowledge: Philosophical Thought in Literary Context', *Journal of Aesthetics and Art Criticism*, 56: 331–48.

KERMODE, FRANK (2000). *Shakespeare's Language*. London: Penguin.

KIERAN, MATTHEW (2005). *Revealing Art*. London: Routledge.

—— (ed.) (2006). *Contemporary Debates in Aesthetics and the Philosophy of Art*. New York: Blackwell.

—— AND LOPES, DOMINIC MCIVER (eds.) (2003). *Imagination, Philosophy, and the Arts*. London: Routledge.

KIVY, PETER (1997). *Philosophies of Arts: An Essay in Differences*. Cambridge: Cambridge University Press.

—— (2006). *The Performance of Reading: An Essay in the Philosophy of Literature*. New York: Blackwell.

KRIPKE, SAUL (1980). *Naming and Necessity*. Cambridge, MA: Harvard University Press.

KRAUSZ, MICHAEL (ed.) (2002). *Is There a Single Right Interpretation?* College Park, PA: Pennsylvania State University Press.

LAMARQUE, PETER (1989). 'Critical Discussion of David Novitz, *Fiction and Imagination*', *Philosophy and Literature*, 13: 365–74.

—— (1996). *Fictional Points of View*. Ithaca, NY: Cornell University Press.

LAMARQUE, PETER AND OLSEN, STEIN HAUGOM (1994). *Truth, Fiction and Literature: A Philosophical Perspective*. Oxford: Clarendon Press.

LEAVIS, F. R. (1967). *Anna Karenina and Other Essays*. London: Routledge.

LEVINSON, JERROLD (ed.) (1998). *Aesthetics and Ethics: Essays at the Intersection*. Cambridge: Cambridge University Press.

—— (ed.) (2003). *Oxford Handbook of Aesthetics*. Oxford: Oxford University Press.

LEWIS, DAVID (1978). 'Truth in Fiction', *American Philosophical Quarterly*, 15: 37–46.

LIVINGSTON, PAISLEY (2005). *Art and Intention: A Philosophical Study*. Oxford: Oxford University Press.

LODGE, DAVID (1996). *The Practice of Writing*. New York: Penguin.

LYOTARD, JEAN-FRANÇOIS (1984). *The Postmodern Condition: A Report on Knowledge*, trans. G. Bennington and B. Massumi. Manchester: Manchester University Press.

MCCARTHY, TIMOTHY, AND STIDD, SEAN STIDD (eds.) (2001). *Wittgenstein in America*. Oxford: Oxford University Press.

MACDONALD, MARGARET (1954). 'The Language of Fiction', *Proceedings of the Aristotelian Society*, 28: 165–84.

MCDOWELL, JOHN (1996). *Mind and World*, 2nd edn. Cambridge, MA: Harvard University Press.

MCHALE, BRIAN (1992). *Constructing Postmodernism*. New York: Routledge.

MILLER, ERIC (1996). 'Is Literature Self-Referential?' *Philosophy and Literature*, 20: 474–86.

MILLER, J. HILLIS (2002). *On Literature*. London: Routledge.

MULHALL, STEPHEN (1994). *Stanley Cavell: Philosophy's Recounting of the Ordinary*. Oxford: Clarendon Press.

—— (ed.) (1996). *The Cavell Reader*. Oxford: Blackwell.

MURDOCH, IRIS (1970). *The Sovereignty of Good*. London: Routledge.

NAGEL, THOMAS (1979). *Mortal Questions*. Cambridge: Cambridge University Press.

NEW, CHRISTOPHER (1996). 'Walton on Imagination, Belief, and Fiction', *British Journal of Aesthetics*, 36: 159–65.

NORRIS, CHRISTOPHER (1982). *Deconstruction: Theory and Practice*. London: Methuen.

NOVITZ, DAVID (1979–80). 'Fiction, Imagination, and Emotion', *Journal of Aesthetics and Art Criticism*, 38: 279–88.
—— (1983). 'Fiction and the Growth of Knowledge', *Grazer Philosophische Studien*, 19: 47–68.
—— (1987). *Knowledge, Fiction and Imagination*. Philadelphia: Temple University Press.
—— (1990). 'Art, Life and Reality', *British Journal of Aesthetics*, 30: 301–10.
—— (1995). 'The Trouble with Truth', *Philosophy of Literature*, 19: 350–9.
NUSSBAUM, MARTHA (1986). *The Fragility of Goodness: Luck and Ethics in Greek Tragedy and Philosophy*. Cambridge: Cambridge University Press.
—— (1990). *Love's Knowledge: Essays on Philosophy and Literature*. Oxford: Oxford University Press.
—— (1995). *Poetic Justice: The Literary Imagination and Public Life*. Boston: Beacon Press.
—— (1998). 'Exactly and Responsibly: A Defense of Ethical Criticism', *Philosophy and Literature*, 22: 343–65.
NUTTALL, A. D. (1983). *A New Mimesis: Shakespeare and the Representation of Reality*. New York: Methuen.
OLSEN, STEIN HAUGOM (1978). *The Structure of Literary Understanding*. Cambridge: Cambridge University Press.
—— (1987). *The End of Literary Theory*. Cambridge: Cambridge University Press.
PATAI, DAPHNE, AND CORRAL, WILL H. (eds.) (2005). *Theory's Empire: An Anthology of Dissent*. New York: Columbia University Press.
PAVEL, THOMAS (1986). *Fictional Worlds*. Cambridge, MA: Harvard University Press.
PEIRCE, CHARLES S. (1960). *Collected Papers*, ed. Charles Hartshorne and Paul Weiss. Cambridge: Belknap.
PETTERSSON, ANDERS (1993). 'On Walton's and Currie's Analyses of Literary Fiction', *Philosophy and Literature*, 17: 84–97.
PLATO (1984). *The Dialogues of Plato*, trans. R. E. Allen. New Haven: Yale University Press.
PUTNAM, HILARY (1975). *Philosophical Papers*, ii. *Mind, Language and Reality*. Cambridge: Cambridge University Press.

PUTNAM, HILARY (1975–6). 'Literature, Science, and Reflection', *New Literary History*, 7: 483–92.

—— (1979). 'Reflections on Goodman's *Ways of Worldmaking*', *Journal of Philosophy*, 76: 603–18.

—— (1983). *Philosophical Papers*, iii. *Realism and Reason*. Cambridge: Cambridge University Press.

—— (1983–4). 'The Craving for Objectivity', *New Literary History*, 15: 229–39.

—— (1987). *The Many Faces of Realism*. LaSalle, ILL: Open Court.

—— (1989). *Representation and Reality*. Cambridge, MA: MIT Press.

—— (1990). *Realism with a Human Face*, ed. James Conant. Cambridge, MA: Harvard University Press.

—— (1994). 'The Dewey Lectures 1994: Sense, Nonsense, and the Senses: An Inquiry into the Powers of the Human Mind', *Journal of Philosophy*, 91: 445–517.

RADFORD, COLIN (1975). 'How Can We Be Moved by the Fate of Anna Karenina?' *Proceedings of the Aristotelian Society*, 69: 67–80.

RORTY, RICHARD (1978). 'Philosophy as a Kind of Writing: An Essay on Derrida', *New Literary History*, 10: 141–60.

—— (1979). *Philosophy and the Mirror of Nature*. Princeton: Princeton University Press.

—— (1982). *Consequences of Pragmatism: Essays 1972–1980*. Minneapolis: University of Minneapolis Press.

—— (1989). *Contingency, Irony, and Solidarity*. Cambridge: Cambridge University Press.

RUSSELL, BERTRAND (1956). *Logic and Knowledge*, ed. R. C. Marsh. London: Routledge.

—— (1962). *An Inquiry into Meaning and Truth*. London: Pelican.

RYLE, GILBERT (1984). *The Concept of Mind*. Chicago: University of Chicago Press.

SAUSSURE, FERDINAND DE (1974). *Course in General Linguistics*, trans. Wade Baskin, rev. edn. London: Routledge.

SCHALKWYK, DAVID (1995). 'Fiction as "Grammatical" Investigation: A Wittgensteinian Account', *Journal of Aesthetics and Art Criticism*, 53: 287–98.

—— (2004). *Literature and the Touch of the Real*. Newark, DEL: University of Delaware Press.

SCHMITT, FREDRICK F. (1995). *Truth: A Primer.* Boulder, CO: Westview Press.
SEARLE, JOHN (1977). 'Reiterating the Difference: A Reply to Derrida', *Glyph*, 1: 198–208.
—— (1979). *Expression and Meaning: Studies in the Theory of Speech Acts.* Cambridge: Cambridge University Press.
—— (1993). 'Is There a Crisis in American Higher Education?' *Partisan Review*, 60/4: 693–709.
SELDEN, RAMAN, AND WIDDOWSON, PETER (1993). *A Reader's Guide to Contemporary Literary Theory.* London: Harvester Wheatsheaf.
SHAKESPEARE, WILLIAM (1992). *Othello*, ed. M. R. Ridley. London: Routledge.
SHUSTERMAN, RICHARD (2001). 'Art as Dramatization', *Journal of Aesthetics and Art Criticism*, 59, 363–72.
STOLNITZ, JEROME (1992). 'On the Cognitive Triviality of Art', *British Journal of Aesthetics*, 32: 191–200.
THOMSON-JONES, KATHERINE (2005). 'Inseparable Insight: Reconciling Cognitivism and Formalism in Aesthetics', *Journal of Aesthetics and Art Criticism*, 63: 375–84.
TODOROV, TZVETAN (2002). *Imperfect Garden: The Legacy of Humanism*, trans. Carol Cosman. Princeton: Princeton University Press.
WALTON, KENDALL (1973). 'Pictures and Make-Believe', *Philosophical Review* 82: 283–319.
—— (1978). 'Fearing Fictions', *Journal of Philosophy* 75: 5–27.
—— (1978–9). 'How Remote Are Fictional Worlds from the Real World?' *Journal of Aesthetics and Art Criticism*, 37: 11–23.
—— 1980). 'Appreciating Fiction: Suspending Belief or Pretending Belief?' *Dispositio*, 5: 1–18.
—— (1990). *Mimesis as Make-Believe.* Cambridge, MA: Harvard University Press.
WESTON, MICHAEL (2001). *Literature, Philosophy and the Human Good.* London: Routledge.
WHITE, HAYDEN (1978). *Tropics of Discourse.* Baltimore: Johns Hopkins University Press.
WILLIAMS, BERNARD (1985). *Ethics and the Limits of Philosophy.* Cambridge, MA: Harvard University Press.
WILLIAMS, MICHAEL (1991). *Unnatural Doubts: Epistemological Realism and the Basis of Scepticism.* Oxford: Blackwell.

WILSON, CATHERINE (1983). 'Literature and Knowledge.' *Philosophy*, 58: 489–96.

WITTGENSTEIN, LUDWIG (1980). *Culture and Value*, ed. G. H. von Wright, trans. P. Winch. Chicago: University of Chicago Press.

____ (2001). *Philosophical Investigations*, 2nd edn., ed. G. E. M Anscombe and R. Rhees, trans. G. E. M. Anscombe. Oxford: Blackwell.

WOLLHEIM, RICHARD (1993). *The Mind and Its Depths*. Cambridge, MA: Harvard University Press.

WRIGHT, CRISPIN (1992). *Truth and Objectivity*. Cambridge, MA: Harvard University Press.

Index

acknowledgement 102–20
Aristotle 13, 15, 19, 69, 82 n. 1, 160, 182
articulation of culture (and interpretation) 142–5
Attridge, D. 51 n. 2
autonomy (literary) 48, 51
axiological understanding 109–10

Barthes, R. 37
Bataille, G. 56 n. 8
Baudrillard, J. 148–9, 150, 174
Beardsley, M. 43, 90 n. 12, 128
Blanchot, M. 56 n. 8
Bloom, H. 76 n., 114
Brooks, C. 14 n. 3, 133, 134, 138

Calvino, I. 33
Carroll, N. 14 n. 2, 102 n. 19, 119, 170–1, 177 n. 37
Cavell, S. 31, 66, 102–3, 104, 105 n. 23, 109, 111 n. 28
cognitive familiarity (the problem of) 83, 99, 112
cognitive value of literature 2, 4, 82–5, 99–102, 112–20
of literary criticism 141–5
conventionalism (interpretive) 126–7
Cooper, D. 124 n. 4
Critchley, S. 58 n. 10
criteria 66–8, 73, 78–9, 84, 108–11, 118–19
critical meaning 124–5, 132–6, and truth 144
Currie, G. 21, 37, 160, 163 n. 24

Davies, D. 158 n. 15

Davies, S. 29 n. 17
Davis, T. 14 n. 2
de Bolla, P. 116 n. 116
de Man, P. 37, 149
deconstruction 37 n. 27, 41, 149–50; *see also* poststructuralism
Derrida, J. 3, 37, 38, 56 n. 8, 149, 150 n. 10, 155
Dickens, C. 138–9
Diffey, T. 23 n. 13, 98–9
Doležel, L. 29, 43, 154, 186
Dostoevsky, F. 26, 71, 72, 74, 113, 118, 138, 184
expressive freedom 143

drama 8, 108, 115
dramatic understanding 108, 115, 116–17
drifts (analytic and poststructuralist) 39–46

Eagleton, T. 14 n. 2, 132–3, 138, 149–50
Eco, U. 41, 45, 142
Eldridge, R. 14 n. 2, 102 n. 102, 131, 143, 182
Elgin, C. 177 n. 37

Farrell, F. 14 n. 2
Faulkner, W. 31, 124, 133, 134, 138
fictional worlds 17, 21, 43–4, 90, 155, 174, 183
meaning of 132–4
connection to reality 136–41
Fish, S. 150
Freeland, C. 14 n. 2
Frege, G. 6, 7, 33, 158

Friend, S. 165

Gaut, B. 14 n. 2, 87 n. 5
Goldie, P. 104 n. 22
Goldman, A. 130 n. 13
Goodman, N. 147
Graham, G. 94
Guetti, J. 72 n. 20

Hammer, E. 102 n. 20, 117 n. 33
Harrison, B. 14 n. 2, 16 n. 7, 42 n. 36, 79, 130, 182 n. 44
humanism (literary) 2, 13–16
  indirect humanism 118–28
  direct humanism 117–18, 129–30
  truth-seeking humanism 86–99
  and interpretation 122, 132, 134, 140

intentionalism (interpretive) 126, 128–9
isolationism (literary) 48–9, 52, 53, 69, 74, 78, 81, 84

John, E. 14 n. 2, 19 n. 8, 121 n. 1, 177 n. 37

Katholou 182
Kieran, M. 14 n. 2
Kivy, P. 97, 131
Krausz, M. 128 n. 8, 131 n. 130
Kripke, S. 64 n. 16
knowledge *see* cognitive value of literature

Lamarque, P. 16 n. 7, 37, 102 n. 20, 122
  and Stein Haugom Olsen 14 n. 2, 21, 32 n. 23, 93, 94, 161
Levinson, J. 128 n. 7
literary value 4–5, 19, 22, 24, 27, 51; *see also* cognitive value of literature

Livingston, P. 128 n. 7

Mailer, N. 31 n. 22
make-believe 18, 44–5, 146, 157–73, 174; *see also* Walton, K.
  canonical version of, 157–8, 163, 170
McDowell, J. 135
Miller, E. 45–6, 47 n. 44
Miller, J. Hillis. 54, 56 n. 8
Mulhall, S. 102 n. 20, 109

New, C. 167
Norris, C. 150 n. 10
Novitz, D. 14 n. 2, 149 n. 5
Nussbaum, M. 14 n. 2, 26 n. 15, 88

panfictionalism 147–57
  'pop' and proper versions 149
Peirce, C. S. 39 n. 31
Pettersson, A. 171
Paif, E. 180
Plato 15–16, 25, 83, 98, 120
Pocci, L. 90 n. 11
Porter, C. 179, 181
poststructuralism 37–42, 149

racism (concept of) 75–9
Rescher, N. 176
Rorty, R. 38, 40 n. 32, 42 n. 37, 58
Russell, B. 43, 131, 158, 159, 163, 164

Schalkwyk, D. 3 n. 1, 79
Sedivy, S. 113 n. 29
Shakespeare, W. 75–9, 124, 129, 181
Shusterman, R. 108 n. 25
standards of representation 63–8; *see also* criteria
  and literature 71–4, 79, 183

stances (fictive and worldly) 122–3, 173–5, 183
Stecker, R. 126 n. 6
Strayhorn, B. 179

textual constraint, the 27–8, 97, 117–18, 140–1
Thomson-Jones, K. 118 n. 34
thought experiments 175–8
truth *see* cognitive value of literature

unclaimed truths, the problem of 93

Walton, K. 37, 44, 157–73; *see also* make-believe
Weston, M. 14 n. 2, 56 n. 8
Williams, M. 68 n. 19
Wilson, C. 20
Wittgenstein, L. 59, 61–5, 107, 176, 177
Wright, C. 57 n. 9